DISCOVERY GUIDE
THE PATH TO THE CROSS

THAT THE WORLD MAY KNOW®

5 FAITH LESSONS™ BY
RAY VANDER LAAN
with Stephen & Amanda Sorenson

ZONDERVAN®   FOCUS ON THE FAMILY®

ZONDERVAN.com/
AUTHORTRACKER
follow your favorite authors

ZONDERVAN

The Path to the Cross Discovery Guide
Copyright © 2010 by Ray Vander Laan

Requests for information should be addressed to:

Zondervan, *Grand Rapids, Michigan 49530*

Focus on the Family and the accompanying logo and design are federally registered trademarks of Focus on the Family, *Colorado Springs, Colorado 80995.*

That the World May Know and Faith Lessons are trademarks of Focus on the Family.

ISBN 978-0-310-32985-5

All maps created by International Mapping.

All photos are courtesy of Ray Vander Laan, Mark Tanis, and Amanda Sorenson.

All illustrations are courtesy of Drew Johnson and Rob Perry.

All Scripture quotations, unless otherwise indicated, are taken from the Holy Bible, *New International Version®, NIV®.* Copyright © 1973, 1978, 1984 by Biblica, Inc.™ Used by permission of Zondervan. All rights reserved worldwide.

Scripture quotations marked MSG are taken from *The Message.* Copyright © 1993, 1994, 1995, 1996, 2000, 2001, 2002. Used by permission of NavPress Publishing Group.

Interior design: Ben Fetterley

Printed in the United States of America

12 13 14 15 /DCI/ 25 24 23 22 21 20 19 18 17 16 15 14 13 12 11 10 9 8 7 6 5

CONTENTS

INTRODUCTION

From the beginning of human history, God the Creator planned to reclaim his world from the chaos of sin. He wanted to restore *shalom* to his creation, and he chose to use people to accomplish this divine purpose. Through the great exodus of the Hebrews from slavery in Egypt to their home in the Promised Land, God revealed himself to his people, gave them their identity as his chosen people, and instructed them in who he wanted them to become and how he wanted them to live.

The whole story of God reaching into human history and redeeming his chosen people to fulfill his redemptive purpose is recorded in the Torah. Thus the Torah forms the foundation of all future acts of God recorded throughout the Bible. It is God's blueprint for the role he desires his people to play in the restoration of *shalom* to his world. It provides the historical, cultural, and redemptive context through which we can better understand the coming of Jesus, the Messiah, and his path to the cross.

God Reclaims His World through the Witness of His People

The Hebrews were to be God's witness to the world of his plan to reclaim his creation. So the exodus of the Hebrew people from Egypt to the Promised Land was more than a compassionate act of divine deliverance. It was God's calling of a people to be his "treasured possession," "kingdom of priests," and "holy nation" who would put him on display for the whole world to see (Exodus 19:4–6). God, in effect, took Israel as his bride, and lived among them through the years of discipline and testing in the desert in order to mold and shape them to be his faithful witnesses to the world.

The mission of God's people today is the same one he gave to his ancient people: to live obediently *within* the world so that through us *the world may know that our God is the one true God.* For this reason, the great, redemptive acts of God revealed in the exodus are central to the stories of both the Hebrew text (Old Testament) and the Christian text (New Testament).

The historical account of the exodus is central to understanding why many followers of Jesus considered him to be the prophet like Moses — the Messiah — whom the Lord had promised to send (Deuteronomy 18:17 - 19; Luke 7:16; 24:19; John 6:14). Jesus often used ideas found in the exodus story, and many of his teachings interpret Moses' words in the Torah. Jesus also positioned his redemptive acts against the background of festivals — Passover, Unleavened Bread, and First Fruit — that are associated with the Hebrews' deliverance from Egypt.[1] And at the deepest level, the exodus story not only provides a background for God's plan to bring Jesus into the world as Messiah, it is one of the first chapters in God's great redemptive story to restore *shalom* — unity, harmony, order — to his broken creation.

For those of us who seek to live as God's people today, it is essential that we understand these stories as more than ancient history. The stories of the Bible describe God and define the faith walk of his people. God's people come to know him by what he does, not by attempting to define him with precise doctrine. God's people come to live the way he desires by remembering, retelling, and reliving his great redemptive acts, not by simply memorizing laws, rules, and regulations.

Despite the many failures of God's people in fulfilling their role in that story, God's power has and continues to flow through his flawed (Jesus excepted, of course) human instruments to bring to fruition his plan of redemption. So, like the ancient Hebrews, we need deliverance from the bondage of Egypt. We need to be amazed by God's power at work at the Red Sea. We need to respond to his voice at Mount Sinai. As we wander through the deserts of our lives, we need to set our feet firmly on the foundation of depending on God and living by his every word. Their story is our story. As we come to know that story and partake of the redemption God offers through his Son, Jesus Christ, we too become part of that ancient story of redemption.

Thus the exodus is a paradigm for our own experience. As Christians today, we can describe our deliverance in similar language because God delivers us by his mercy and the protecting blood of the Lamb — Jesus Christ. Without the exodus, we would not be who we are — redeemed people delivered by the God of Israel. And without the hardships of the desert experience, we would find it difficult to learn how to live in intimate dependence on his provision and by faithful obedience to his every word.

God Reveals His Story through the Language of Culture

Although the message of God's story is eternal and unchanging, the writings through which God has revealed himself clearly bear the stamp of time and place. The circumstances and conditions of the people of the Bible are unique to their times. So God has spoken through the context of the cultures in which his people lived. He has used the familiar images of daily life as a means to communicate his message.

For example, when Abraham made a blood covenant with God, he sacrificed animals in a way similar to that of the neighboring Hittites. The staff Moses used symbolized God's power in ways similar to the "stick" that represented Pharaoh's power in countless statues and carvings throughout Egypt. The tabernacle bears an uncanny resemblance to the war camp of Pharaoh Ramses. The temple Solomon built in Jerusalem is similar in design to the temples of neighboring cultures.

So it should not surprise us that Jesus spoke and acted within the context of the culture of his day. He experienced life in the first century as a Jew from Nazareth. He lived in a land dominated by harsh Roman overlords and corrupt religious leaders. His sandaled feet got dirty. He knew the hard work of a builder or stonemason. He worshipped in the synagogues of Galilee and the temple at Jerusalem. He experienced hunger and thirst under the burning sun of the Judea Wilderness. As he fulfilled his role in God's great redemptive story, his words, actions, and teaching methods were in keeping with the traditions and practices of the Jewish culture in which he lived.

The religious and cultural identity of the Jewish people of Jesus' day was rooted in the exodus experience. Jesus often quoted the Torah and identified himself as the prophet and king promised in it. Thus the desert experiences on which this study will focus provide a context for better understanding God's great redemptive plan and the life and ministry of Jesus.

Although we cannot consider all (or even many) of the significant connections between the ministry of Jesus and the Hebrews' desert wanderings, we will consider enough to start shaping a picture of Jesus and his world in light of the exodus. We will see how the Essenes and John the Baptist are linked to the desert experiences of Israel's past. We will follow Jesus into the desert where he, like Israel, was tested and prepared for his mission to the world. Finally we will consider the events of the Last Supper and the night of watching in Gethsemane against the backdrop of the exodus experience.

Clarifying Our Terminology

In this study, the record of God's reclaiming and restoring his broken world is called the Bible, Scripture, or the "text." Having studied in the Jewish world, I believe it is important to communicate clearly how the nature of that inspired book is understood. Although it can be helpful to speak of Scripture in terms of Old and New Testaments, these descriptions also can be misleading if they are interpreted to mean old and outdated in contrast to a new replacement. Nothing, in my opinion, is further from the truth.

Whereas the "New Testament" describes the great advance of God's plan with the arrival of the Messiah and the promise of his completed and continuing work, the "Old Testament" describes the foundational events and people through whom God began that work. The Bible is not complete without both Testaments; it comprises God's one revelation, his one plan to reclaim his world and restore harmony between himself and humankind. To emphasize that unity, I prefer to refer to the Hebrew text (Old Testament) and the Christian text (New Testament) that together are the inspired, infallible Word of God.

The geography of the lands of the Bible — Egypt, the desert, the Promised Land — shaped the people who lived there, and biblical writers assumed that their readers were familiar with the culture of that world. Many Christians today, however, lack even a basic geographical knowledge of the region and know even less of the ancient cultures that flourished there. So understanding the Scriptures involves more than knowing what the words mean. It also means becoming familiar with the everyday experiences and images the text employs to reveal God's message so that we can begin to understand it from the perspective of the people to whom it originally was given.

For example, the ancient Hebrew people to whom God revealed himself described their world in concrete terms. Their language was one of pictures, metaphors, and examples rather than ideas, definitions, and abstractions. Whereas we might describe God as omniscient or omnipresent (knowing everything and present everywhere), they would describe him as "my Shepherd." Thus the Bible is filled with concrete images from Hebrew culture: God is our Father and we are his children, God is the Potter and we are the clay, Jesus is the Lamb killed on Passover, heaven is an oasis in the desert, and hell is the city sewage dump.

Many of the Bible's images occur first during the exodus: Israel as God's bride, God as shepherd, the desert as a metaphor for life's difficult experiences, God as living water, God as King, God carrying his people on eagle's wings, the saving blood of the lamb. The Hebrews experienced these and many more familiar images as they left Egypt, spent forty years in the desert, and then entered the Promised Land.

The text frequently describes the people themselves, the descendants of Abraham, as "Hebrews," which probably originated from the Egyptian *habiru* meaning "dusty ones" (a reference to their desert origins). Genesis refers to Abraham as "the Hebrew" (Genesis 14:13), and after God gave Jacob the name *Israel*, the text also calls his descendants *Israelites*. The term *Jew* came into use later in history (see the books of Nehemiah and Esther) and was the predominant term used during the time of Jesus.

The Hebrew text refers to the land God promised to Abraham as *Canaan* or *Israel*. The Christian text calls it *Judea*. After the Second Jewish Revolt (AD 132 – 135), it was known as *Palestine*. Each of these names resulted from historical events that took place in the land at the time the terms were coined.

One of the earliest designations of the Promised Land was *Canaan*. It probably meant "purple," referring to the dye produced in the region from the shells of murex shellfish, the people who produced the dye, and the resulting purple cloth that was worn by royalty in the ancient world. In the Bible, *Canaanite* refers to a "trader" or "merchant" (Zechariah 14:21), as well as to a person from the "land of purple," or Canaan.

Israel, another designation for the Promised Land, derives from the patriarch Jacob. His descendants were known as the Hebrews or the children of Israel. After they conquered Canaan during the time of Joshua, the name of the people, *Israel*, became the designation for the land itself (in the same way it had with the Canaanites). When the nation split following the death of Solomon, the name Israel was applied to the territory of the northern kingdom, while the southern land was called Judah. After the northern kingdom fell to the Assyrians in 722 BC, the entire land was again called Israel.

During the time of Jesus, the land that had been the nation of Judah was called *Judea* (which means "Jewish"). The Romans divided the land into several provinces: Judea, Samaria, and Galilee (the three main divisions during Jesus' time); Gaulanitis, the Decapolis, and Perea (east of the Jordan River); and Idumaea (Edom) and Nabatea (in the south). About one hundred years after Jesus' death, the Roman emperor Hadrian called the land *Palestine* in an effort to eliminate Jewish influence in the area.

Today the names *Israel* and *Palestine* are often used to designate the land God gave to Abraham. Both terms are politically charged. *Palestine* is used by Arabs living in the central part of the country, and *Israel* is used by Jews to indicate the political State of Israel. In this study, *Israel* is used in the biblical sense. This does not indicate a political statement regarding the current struggle in the Middle East but best reflects the biblical designation for the land.

Establishing the Historic and Geographic Setting for Events Recorded in the Text

When studying the exodus of the Hebrews from Egypt, it is natural to ask, "When did that event occur?" or, "Who was the Pharaoh who did not know about Joseph?" (Exodus 1:8). Of the two basic theories,[2] one places the biblical event in the eighteenth Egyptian dynasty around 1450 BC during the reign of Pharaohs such as Thutmose (3) or Amenhotep (2)[3] and the other places it during the nineteenth dynasty during the reign of Ramses the Great (1279 – 1213 BC).[4] Significant textual and scientific support exists for each perspective.

I have my opinion, but this study in no way argues for one position or the other. Since the Bible does not name the Pharaoh (a word similar to "king" in English), God apparently did not believe this fact to be central to his message. However, in much the same way that one studies ancient languages or uses a good commentary, it is helpful to study specific cultural settings in order to better understand the biblical text. This study focuses on Pharaoh Ramses the Great because he was the epitome of all Pharaohs. Whoever the Pharaoh of the exodus was, we can be sure he wanted and tried to be like Ramses.

I hold a similar position regarding the route of the exodus. There are many proposed routes, and I do not seek to support one over another. I have chosen for this study the type of terrain and culture that would represent whichever route the Hebrews took. The foundational position for this study is that the exodus and other biblical events occurred as the Bible describes them. My desire is to provide a sense of the culture of the time and place of these events without adding the burden of controversy regarding specific dates and locations.

The message of the Scriptures is eternal and unchanging, and the mission of God's people remains the same, but the circumstances of the people of the Bible are unique to their times. Consequently, we most clearly understand God's truth when we know the cultural context within which he spoke and acted and the perception of the people with whom he communicated. This does not mean that God's revelation is unclear if we don't know the cultural context. Rather, by cultivating our understanding of the world in which God's story was told, we will begin to see it as an actual place with real people and a real culture.

As we explore and study the people and events of the Bible in their geographical and historical contexts, we will discover the *who*, *what*, and *where* of God's redemptive work through human history and will better understand the *why*. By learning how to think and approach life as Abraham, Moses, Joshua, Elijah, Esther, John the Baptist, and other people through whom God worked, we will deepen our appreciation for God's story. We will become more familiar with the world and culture of God's ancient people. We will seek to better understand God's revealed mission for them so that we, in turn, will better understand God's purpose and more fully apply the Bible's message to our lives.

Our purpose is to follow God's intent as revealed to Ezekiel:

> *Son of man, look with your eyes and hear with your ears and pay attention to everything I am going to show you, for that is why you have been brought here. Tell the house of Israel everything you see.*
>
> **Ezekiel 40:4**

So come, look and see. Then go and live in such a way that all the world will come to know God as the one, true God.

THE WAY OF THE ESSENES

About 150 years before the birth of Jesus the Messiah, some of God's people — the Essenes — established a community in the Judea Wilderness near the northern end of the Dead Sea. We know it as Qumran, where the Dead Sea Scrolls were found. Not all scholars agree that Essenes lived at Qumran, wrote the Dead Sea Scrolls, or were the people the scrolls portray, so study and debate about the nature of the community continue. However, given the lack of other significant theories about Qumran, the scrolls, and the Essenes, we will take the position of mainstream Bible scholars that the Qumran ruins are those of the Dead Sea Scroll community that was part of a religious movement that included the Essenes.

In any case, our primary focus is not on the relationship between the people who lived in this community and the Dead Sea Scrolls. We will focus on why this group of God's people went into the desert to live as they did. We want to know the role they played in God's great story of redemption.

Part of the answer is revealed in the Hebrew Bible where the prophets proclaimed God's command for his people to "prepare the way" for his coming. Malachi wrote that God would come after he sent his messenger to prepare his way (Malachi 3:1). The words of Isaiah add further insight: "In the desert prepare the way for the Lord; make straight in the wilderness a highway for our God" (Isaiah 40:3).

THE ESSENES SPENT LONG HOURS IN THE BRUTAL DESERT HEAT WRITING ON PARCHMENT. THEIR WRITINGS INCLUDED BOOKS FROM THE HEBREW BIBLE, COMMENTARIES ON THESE BOOKS, AND THE REGULATIONS OF THE ESSENE COMMUNITY.

The Essenes were passionately committed to learning and obeying every word that came from the mouth of God. They knew that God wanted to dwell among them and believed with all their heart, soul, and strength that if they prepared the way he would come. So they eagerly anticipated the coming of the Messiah and went into the desert to "prepare the way" for him.

But anyone who has hiked the rugged mountains of the Judea Wilderness will likely ask, "Why did the way for God have to be prepared *in the desert*, especially this one?" Throughout history this wilderness has remained virtually uninhabited. Its rough, steep terrain and lack of water make it unsuitable for good travel routes. Its summer heat frequently exceeds 120 degrees Fahrenheit, hot winds often dry out any remaining moisture, and chilling temperatures set in soon after sunset.

Wouldn't it have been easier for God's way to be prepared in the fertile countryside near the Sea of Galilee or the well-watered hillsides near Jerusalem? Why did God choose the desert as the place for his people to prepare for his glory to be revealed? Why did he choose a place where simply surviving is so hard?

Again, part of the answer can be found in the Hebrew Bible. In the exodus story, God worked through his prophet Moses to miraculously bring the Hebrews out of slavery in Egypt, deliver them from Pharaoh's army at the Red Sea, and lead them into the "vast and dreadful desert" (Deuteronomy 8:15) where he met with them and lived among them for forty years. In the desert, they learned to depend on God and live by his every word. Isolated from the influence of Egyptian and Canaanite cultures, the Israelites became a unified people whom God molded and shaped to be a kingdom of priests who would display his character to the world.

In a sense, the desert is the perfect place for God's people (including us today) to learn to be his people. In the desert, the diversions of a comfortable lifestyle fade into silence, and God's powerful whisper can be heard. In the desert, we can survive — and even

THE ESSENES LEFT UPPER-CLASS LIFESTYLES FOR HUTS IN THE HARSH WILDERNESS OF JUDEA, A MEASURE OF THEIR EXTREME DEVOTION TO THE BIBLE. THE ESSENE MEMBERS WERE MALE, HOWEVER THERE IS EVIDENCE THAT THEY LIVED IN THE DESERT WITH THEIR FAMILIES AS THEY PREPARED THE LORD'S WAY OF OBEDIENCE.

thrive — but only by God's faithful provision. In the desert, we learn that it is better to be in the arms of God during tough circumstances than to rest in paradise and forget about him. In the desert, the influence of gods of our own making lose their power, and we are drawn into intimate relationship with the one true God.

So we should not be surprised to find the Essenes in the desert. There, for weeks, months, years — and sometimes a lifetime — they exchanged lives of relative comfort for desert hardships in order to live out their passionate commitment to obey every word that came from the mouth of God. There, they created a community isolated from the self-focused, pleasure-seeking Hellenistic society and what had become a corrupt priesthood in Jerusalem. In the desert they dedicated themselves to preparing the way for God.

And out of that same barren desert, the Bible character we know as John the Baptist took up the cry. With the fiery passion of Elijah, he called on sinners to repent and prepare the way for the Lord. And just as the prophets had said, God came as Jesus the Messiah to continue the next chapter in God's great redemptive story.

Opening Thoughts (3 minutes)

The Very Words of God

> A voice of one calling:
> "In the desert prepare
>   the way for the LORD;
> make straight in the wilderness
>   a highway for our God.
> Every valley shall be raised up,
>   every mountain and hill made low;
> the rough ground shall become level,
>   the rugged places a plain.
> And the glory of the LORD will be revealed,
> and all mankind together will see it.
>   For the mouth of the LORD has spoken."

Isaiah 40:3 – 5

Think About It

Take a few moments to think about your image of what it means to love God and live for him, then describe what you think a life of passionate obedience and faithful devotion to God looks like.

What sacrifices might be required in order to obey God and love him with all our heart, soul, and strength?

DVD Notes (29 minutes)

God shapes and molds his people in the desert

The Essene community: learning to live by God's every word

The Essene lifestyle: passionate obedience and intense devotion

Prepare the way for the Lord

DVD Discussion (7 minutes)

1. At times God chose to use harsh desert areas near the Promised Land as a training ground to mold and shape his people
   for their role in the next chapter of his unfolding story. Like
   a shepherd, he led the ancient Israelites through the deserts
   of the Sinai Peninsula to teach them to depend on him and
   live by his every word. Moses and Elijah spent time with God
   in the Sinai deserts. Elijah, David, John the Baptist, and Jesus
   spent time with God in the Judea Wilderness. The Essenes
   went into that same wilderness to prepare the way of the
   Lord — to know his words and obediently "walk" his path.

   On the map on page 21, locate the Dead Sea, Jerusalem,
   Hebron, Bethlehem, En Gedi, Qumran, and Jericho. Next
   locate specific desert areas in the region: Judea Wilderness
   (Judah Wilderness in Old Testament times), Desert of Zin,
   Negev, Desert of Paran, Desert of Sin, Desert of Shur. How
   far was the Judea Wilderness from Jerusalem? From Bethlehem?

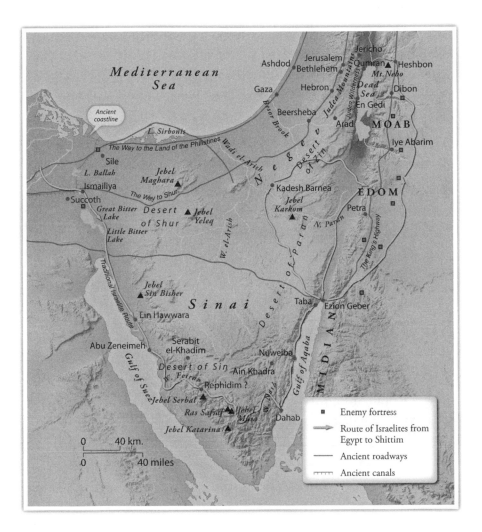

2. What new insights into the Essenes and their lifestyle did
    you discover as you watched the video?

In what ways does the Essenes' level of dedication, commitment, and faithfulness in seeking to obey every word of God make an impact on you?

How does the extent of their personal sacrifice help you to comprehend how much they valued the opportunity to participate in preparing the way for the coming of the Lord?

3. In what way(s) do you think the desert wilderness setting helped to fulfill the deep spiritual commitments that defined the Essene community?

4. Do you think the Essenes could have accomplished their objectives in a more hospitable environment? Why or why not?

Small Group Bible Discovery and Discussion (15 minutes)

The Path of Obedience

God brought the ancient Hebrews into the desert to teach them how to obey his words and, by their obedience to his words, to walk in his ways. His words were so important that he instructed Moses to write down all of them in the Torah (Deuteronomy 31:9 – 13). God also instructed his people to return to the desert — either literally or by recalling the Hebrews' time there — in order to remember (obey) his every word and to prepare the way (or path) for his coming.

The Essenes acted on these words. They dedicated themselves to walking the path of obedience. With great passion for obeying God, they willingly endured the desert hardships in order to learn to live by his every word. They had an intense desire to prepare the way for their God in the desert, and their faithful obedience greatly impacted their world. It helped to prepare people to more easily understand and apply the teachings of Jesus and influenced the

A DESERT PATH NEAR QUMRAN IN THE JUDEA WILDERNESS PROVIDES AN IMAGE OF THE DESIRE AND COMMITMENT REQUIRED TO WALK THE PATH OF OBEDIENCE AND "PREPARE THE WAY" FOR GOD.

theological climate of the Jews for about two hundred years. Let's consider what it means to walk the path of obedience and "prepare the way" for God.

1. The discipline of desert life may seem especially harsh to us. So to better understand the way of the Essenes, it will be helpful to revisit why God allowed the ancient Israelites to experience hard times in the desert. From God's perspective, how important was it — and how great a price was it worth — for his people to learn to live by his every word? (See Deuteronomy 8:2 – 3.)

FOR GREATER UNDERSTANDING: THE "WAY OF THE LORD"

Writers of the ancient Hebrew text used concrete language to describe God and the character he expects of his people. They frequently used *halak* ("walk") and *derekh* ("path" or "way") to describe a person's daily life and relationship with God. So rather than saying "Live a good life" as Westerners might say, a writer of the biblical text might say something like "Walk a good walk" or "Walk in the path."

For the Israelites, walking was the primary means of transportation. Sometimes walking was hard and sometimes it was easy. A person could choose one path or another. So the Israelites readily understood what it meant to "walk in the way." Just as we choose a path when we "walk" from one place to another, we choose a lifestyle "path" as we journey through life. The Bible describes an obedient and righteous lifestyle as "God's path" or the "way of the LORD" (Genesis 18:19) and a rebellious and sinful lifestyle as our "own way" (Isaiah 53:6) or "the way of the wicked" (Psalm 1:6).

In addition to meaning "path," *derekh* can refer to a major road or a path that is worn by constant walking. The word is also translated "obedience" and "commands." So when God told his people to walk in his "ways" as he had taught them, he wanted them to learn to walk his right path or road by obeying his commands. To walk in the *way of the Lord* is to obey his words.

God, too, has a *derekh* (Isaiah 40:3). If we desire to walk with God, he wants us to prepare his way—his path—by walking obediently in it. The Essenes went into the desert to prepare the *derekh,* or way, of the Lord. They prepared the way by walking in his path, which they accomplished by obeying his every word.

2. When Moses recorded how God wanted his people to live, he repeatedly told them to walk in the way God had taught them. As you read the following portions of the text, take note of *how* God's people are to walk in his ways. Then discuss specific examples of what it might look like for God's people today to follow these instructions.

Deuteronomy Text	What Does It Mean to Walk in God's Way?
5:32–33	Walk in obedience to all God has commanded you
8:6	Revere him
10:12–13	w/ all your heart + all your soul
26:17	You will listen to God
28:1–2, 9	obey + he will set you above all nations
30:16	obey + you will live + increase + bless you

3. What motivated the Essenes to live as they did in the desert? Part of the answer is found in Isaiah 40:3 – 8, which should be especially meaningful in light of what you have learned about walking in the way of the Lord.

    a. What did Isaiah call God's people to do?

    Prepare a way for the Lord

    b. Where are God's people to do it?

    make a highway for our God

    c. How would you expect God's people to accomplish their task, and what is central to walking in God's path?

    be faithful + Tell others of the Glory of God

    d. In light of this, why do you think that the Essenes wrote and/or collected the Dead Sea Scrolls, many of which are copies of books of the Hebrew Bible or studies of these books?

    To preserve God's word

DATA FILE
The Dead Sea Scrolls: An Accidental Discovery

In 1947, near an old ruin in the Judea Wilderness at the northern end of the Dead Sea, a Bedouin shepherd noticed a small opening to a cave. After throwing a stone into the opening and hearing pottery breaking, he told two family members about his discovery. The next day, Muhammed edh-Dhib squeezed into the cave, which was littered with broken pottery and held ten intact jars.

Two of the intact jars contained a large scroll and two smaller ones, which Muhammed showed to other shepherds. Little did they know that they had just discovered incredible treasures—the book of Isaiah, the *Manual of Discipline* (describing Qumran community rules), and a commentary on the book of Habakkuk! Muhammed hung the scrolls from his tent pole for several months, then sold them to an antiquities dealer named Kando in Bethlehem.

Kando found the cave, located additional scrolls, and then—after showing them to church officials in Jerusalem—sold the three original scrolls to a Jerusalem antiquities dealer named Samuel for less than one hundred

THE CAVES OF QUMRAN

continued on next page . . .

dollars. As word of the discovery spread, Professor E. L. Sukenik of Hebrew University purchased Kando's additional scrolls. Meanwhile, Samuel had taken the three scrolls to the United States where Dr. Sukenik's son, Yigael Yadin, purchased the original find for $250,000. He presented the scrolls to the State of Israel, and they remain in the Israel Museum in Jerusalem.

Bedouin from Muhammed edh-Dhib's tribe located more caves containing additional scrolls and thousands of fragments. An official archaeological investigation was launched to examine the caves and the nearby ruins that scholars recognized as Qumran.

Known today as the Dead Sea Scrolls, these scrolls (mostly scroll fragments) were found in at least eleven caves near the ruins of Qumran. Among the six hundred scrolls represented, scholars have identified copies of all Old Testament books except Esther; Jewish writings from other sources such as the apocryphal book of *Jubilees*; and specific Qumran community writings that included Old Testament commentaries, liturgical writing such as hymns, and rules for community conduct. The most well-known scrolls include the nearly intact Isaiah scroll; the Copper Scroll describing sixty-four locations where temple treasures were hidden (none of which have been found); the Habakkuk commentary in which prophecies of God's judgment are applied to the Romans and those who resisted the Essenes' beliefs; and the *Manual of Discipline* describing Essene community rules.

The Dead Sea Scrolls have profoundly affected our understanding of biblical texts and affirmed the accuracy of the Scriptures. Prior to these discoveries, the oldest copies of the Hebrew Bible dated to approximately AD 1000. These scrolls go back beyond 100 BC. Scholars were amazed to find few differences between old and new texts—most involved spelling changes. Truly, "All Scripture is God-breathed and is useful for teaching, rebuking, correcting and training in righteousness" (2 Timothy 3:16). In addition, the scrolls have provided striking insights into the theological and cultural setting of Jesus' life, the early church, and the history of Judaism.

Faith Lesson (5 minutes)

God led the ancient Hebrews into the desert so that they would learn to walk the right paths — his paths — by faithful obedience to his "words." His inspired words have remained central to the shaping and molding of his people. His words were essential to the walk of the Essenes, they were essential to the walk of Jesus, and they are essential to those of us who seek to follow him today. God's words are so important that when Jesus faced Satan's temptations in the desert, he repeatedly said, "It is written" (Matthew 4:4, 7, 10) and then quoted the very words God gave to the ancient Hebrews in the desert!

1. What does Jesus' response to Satan's temptations reveal to you about the foundational importance of the lessons of the exodus? *That He was learned in God's Word*

2. Try to imagine how highly Jesus valued God's words and how deeply committed he was to walk faithfully on God's path.

    a. What kind of attitude and energy do you imagine Jesus brought to his study of God's words? What do you think was foremost in his mind and heart as he studied God's words and set out to obey them?

        great concentration + reverence — love for God

    b. Describe what living out a commitment to obeying every word from the mouth of God might have looked like in Jesus' daily life and what it might look like for you.

3. Consider what you have learned about the fire in the soul of the Essenes that drove them into the desert to make whatever sacrifices necessary to walk with God and obey his word. In what ways might their example inspire you to make similar sacrifices?

What would those sacrifices be?

In what ways would you expect your life to be different if you, following the example of the Essenes and Jesus, devoted yourself to obeying God's Word and walking in his way?

To what extent are you sold out enough to God and to his Word to make the sacrifices required to walk the path of obedience and prepare the way of the Lord?

Closing (1 minute)

Read together Deuteronomy 28:9 – 10: "The LORD will establish you as his holy people, as he promised you on oath, if you keep the commands of the LORD your God and walk in his ways. Then all the peoples on earth will see that you are called by the name of the LORD."

Then pray together, testifying to God and to one another of your desire to walk in God's ways. Ask God for the strength to fulfill your commitment to learn and obey his every word. Ask him to bless your walk so that other people will come to know him.

Memorize

The Lord will establish you as his holy people, as he promised you on oath, if you keep the commands of the Lord your God and walk in his ways. Then all the peoples on earth will see that you are called by the name of the Lord.

Deuteronomy 28:9–10

Learning to Walk in the Way of the Lord

In-Depth Personal Study Sessions

Day One | The Desert as God's Land

The Very Words of God

> Be careful that you do not forget the LORD your God, failing to observe
> his commands, his laws and his decrees.... He led you through the vast
> and dreadful desert, that thirsty and waterless land, with its venomous
> snakes and scorpions. He brought you water out of hard rock. He gave
> you manna to eat in the desert, something your fathers had never
> known, to humble and to test you so that in the end it might go well
> with you.
>
> Deuteronomy 8:11, 15 – 16

Bible Discovery

The Desert: Where God Teaches His People

God has often used desert settings to test and train, shape and mold
his people. In the desert, he spoke to the patriarchs and established
his covenant through which the entire world would experience his
blessings. In the desert, he established the twelve tribes of Israel, the
priesthood, the worship practices, and the annual celebrations of his
faithfulness and call to obedience. In the desert, God spoke to his
people through Moses — the first great prophet and the prefigure-
ment of the greater Moses to come (Acts 3:17 - 23).

God's ancient people often experienced painful struggle and suffering in the desert, but there they also experienced his faithful provision, mercy, and forgiveness. In the desert they rebelled against God
and then turned to him in repentance and obedient submission.
There, God kindled within his people the desire to know (experience) him, obey (love) him, and trust him completely as his holy
people.

Israel's desert experiences played a formative, foundational role in their becoming the faithful people God desired them to be, and those experiences continue to influence God's people today. The "desert" is not just a difficult place through which we pass; it has a powerful influence on our daily lives and identity as God's people. When we stray from his "path," God calls us back to the faithfulness that his people learned in the desert. By returning to the desert — physically or through the events recorded in Scripture — God's people can rededicate themselves to being God's instruments in the coming of his kingdom. So take a closer look at the land God has chosen to train and shape his people.

1. Read the Bible's descriptions of the desert into which God led his people. Then picture yourself living in or traveling (on foot, of course) through the desert lands of Israel and the Sinai Peninsula. (See Exodus 15:22 - 23; 16:3; 17:1; Numbers 21:4 - 6; Deuteronomy 1:19; 8:15; Isaiah 30:6; Jeremiah 2:6.)

   a. What do you imagine daily life in such a desert would be like? What daily challenges do you think would consume your time and energy, and how hard might it be for you to meet those challenges? What would happen if you failed?

   b. If you lived in such a desert, how might your desires and motivations change? What might be your worries, fears, or temptations?

PROFILE OF DESERT LANDS NEAR AND IN ISRAEL

Sinai Desert. This severe desert has intense daytime heat, chilling nights, and little or no rainfall. Travel across it is difficult due to ridges of steep, rocky mountains. Today a few nomads eke out an existence here caring for flocks and trading with farmers from fertile areas, but to support large numbers of people would require outside resources or God's miraculous provision in order to survive. This desert's inhospitable conditions are highlighted in Deuteronomy 1:19; 8:15; and Psalm 78:40; 107:4–5.

Negev Desert. Barely forty miles south of Jerusalem, this desert can be divided into three distinct regions. With rolling hills and broad valleys, the

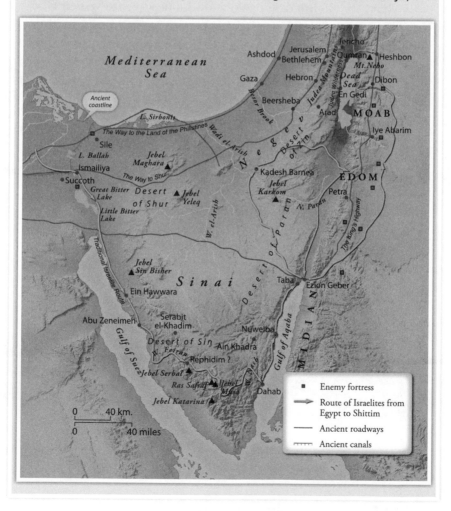

northern region is good sheep country and produces small amounts of grain during a rain-blessed (eight-inch) year. The central region, including the Zin Wilderness, has rugged canyons and is inhospitable even to nomads. The southern region, called the Wilderness of Paran, is the most barren and may receive only two inches of rainfall annually.

The nomadic patriarchs (Abraham, Isaac, Jacob) lived in the Negev, along the edge of fertile farming areas to the north. They traveled great distances seeking pasture and water for their flocks. The small cities in the north were mostly trading posts and military outposts. Here God "partnered" with Abraham and his family so that "all peoples on earth" would be blessed. (See Genesis 12:1–3; 20:1.)

Wilderness of Judea. This desert is on the eastern slope of the Judea Mountains. Roughly ten miles wide and thirty miles long, it begins within a half mile of the well-watered central mountains of Bethlehem and Jerusalem. The mountainous terrain descends suddenly from 3,000 feet above sea

THIS PHOTOGRAPH WAS TAKEN EAST OF BETHLEHEM AT THE VERY WESTERN EDGE OF THE JUDEA WILDERNESS. THE OLIVE GROVES IN THE FOREGROUND PRODUCE A SIGNIFICANT CROP WITHOUT IRRIGATION. IN THE DISTANCE YOU CAN SEE THE RUGGED HILLS IN THE CENTER OF THIS DESERT.

continued on next page . . .

level to 1,400 feet below sea level at the Dead Sea in the Rift Valley, and the dramatic change in altitude creates a "rain shadow." There is just enough rain along the western mountain ridge of this desert for shepherds to pasture their flocks, but the farther east one travels, the more arid the land becomes.

Amazingly, this desert is within sight of anyone living in Israel's central mountains. A person could leave a populated area where crops are grown without the benefit of irrigation and within minutes be in this desert, so it became a refuge for those seeking solitude or safety. Here David hid from Saul, John the Baptist and the Essenes isolated themselves from the usual religious practices of the day in order to focus on God's words, and Jesus faced the evil one. Many biblical events occurred in this desert (1 Samuel 24:1–22; 26:1–25; Psalm 63).

2. Why did God take the Hebrews, whom he had just delivered from Egyptian slavery, into the desert where they experienced a different kind of pain and suffering? (See Exodus 13:17–18; Deuteronomy 8:2–3; Ezekiel 20:8–12.)

3. What specific things did God want his people to learn about their relationship with him through their desert experiences? (See Exodus 16:2–3, 11–12; 29:45–46; Numbers 15:37–41; Deuteronomy 4:33–40; 8:6–18.)

4. In what ways do you think the Israelites' desert experiences prepared them for their role in God's redemptive plan? (See Deuteronomy 4:1 – 9; Isaiah 43:1, 3, 10 – 12.)

THINK ABOUT IT
The Legacy of the Desert

The time the Hebrews spent preparing for the exodus and enduring the desert hardships proved pivotal for their religious faith. Despite their struggles and failures, God revealed to them everything they were to believe and practice. Consider the following examples of the practices God established in the desert and the role these practices played in preparing God's people for the Messiah's arrival. Identify as many links as possible between these practices and Jesus and his ministry.

The Text	The Faith Practice	The Text	The Faith Practice
Ex. 12:1 – 20, 43 – 49	Passover laws	Lev. 11	Clean and unclean food
Ex. 13:3 – 10	Feast of Unleavened Bread	Lev. 16	Day of Atonement
Ex. 20:1 – 17	Ten Commandments	Lev. 23:4 – 43	Feasts of the Lord
Ex. 25 – 30	Tabernacle	Lev. 25:1 – 5	Sabbath rest
Lev. 1 – 7	Offerings to God	Num. 6:1 – 21	The Nazirite
Lev. 8; 21; Num. 6:22 – 26	Priests' ordination and rules	Deut. 6:1 – 19	Love God: keep his commandments

5. It is important to remember that the exodus experience
    was a journey — a time of testing, a time of failure, a time of
    rebellion, a time of submission, a time of teaching, a time
    of maturity. As you read the following portions of the text,
    compare the Israelites' struggles and rebellion with their
    growing faith and commitment to obey God and walk in all
    his ways. In each instance, notice how God responded and
    how his people responded, then describe what you see hap-
    pening in the relationship between God and his people.

Text	God's Action/ Response	The People's Action/Response	The Nature of the Relationship
Ex. 14:10–14, 26–31			
Ex. 15:22–27			
Ex. 16:1–6, 13–30, 35			
Ex. 17:1–7			
Ex. 19:3–8; 32:1–4			
Ex. 39:32–43; 40:33–38; Num. 9:18–23			
Josh. 1:1–5, 10–11; 3:14–17			

DID YOU KNOW?

The Three "Lands" of the Exodus

In a sense, the three geographical regions of the exodus represent the story of all God's people.

Egypt was Pharaoh's land, where the people were in bondage to the security, food, and moral standards that they thought Pharaoh "provided."

The desert was God's land, where Israel learned that God alone met all their needs and trained them to live as his treasured possession.

The Promised Land (Canaan) was the land God gave to Israel as their inheritance to use in obedience to him rather than trusting in their own strength or the false hope of other gods.

As followers of Jesus, we also share in this story. We, too, have been freed from the bondage of sin, led through difficult "deserts" where we learn to obey and depend on God alone, and received blessings from God that he desires us to use in faithful obedience to him.

Reflection

Although we might think of the desert as a place of punishment, God used (and continues to use) it as an ideal place of training and learning. In the desert, God's people depended on him for their survival; he had their full attention. As they came to know and trust him, he transformed his people from oppressed refugees into a powerful nation that was prepared to live by (obey) his every word in the Promised Land. In fact, most of their later triumphs in God's service were rooted in their desert education.

Think about your own "desert" experiences — times of pain and struggle. How do you respond when you are in the "desert"?

Do you remember God's faithfulness and patiently wait for him to provide for your needs (food, guidance, comfort, forgiveness)? Or are you more inclined to become bitter?

Do you turn toward God to seek a deeper, more trusting and obedient relationship with him? Or do you try to run away from him or handle the hardship on your own?

Do you consider your response to the "desert" experiences of your life to be a failure? Why or why not?

How might the ways in which God demonstrated his love and faithfulness to the ancient Hebrews in the desert help you to know and trust him — and depend on him alone?

To what extent are you willing to accept God's instruction (to obey his every word) and mature in your faith as the ancient Hebrews did through their desert experience?

Memorize

> *Be careful that you do not forget the* Lord *your God, failing to observe his commands, his laws and his decrees.... He led you through the vast and dreadful desert, that thirsty and waterless land, with its venomous snakes and scorpions. He brought you water out of hard rock. He gave you manna to eat in the desert, something your fathers had never known, to humble and to test you so that in the end it might go well with you.*
>
> Deuteronomy 8:11, 15 – 16

Day Two | Remember the Desert

The Very Words of God

> *Remember how the* Lord *your God led you all the way in the desert these forty years, to humble you and to test you in order to know what was in your heart, whether or not you would keep his commands. He humbled you, causing you to hunger and then feeding you with manna, which neither you nor your fathers had known, to teach you that man does not live on bread alone but on every word that comes from the mouth of the* Lord.
>
> Deuteronomy 8:2 – 3

Bible Discovery

Remember and Obey the Lessons of the Desert

It is easy for us to think about the exodus in terms of its impact on the ancient Israelites. In the desert, God revealed his intimate presence to them through fire, cloud, and the thunder of his voice. His awesome miracles — water gushing out of rock, bread and meat from heaven, deliverance from enemies — testified to his love and protection over his beloved people. Of course God wanted them to remember all that he had done and to obey all of his words.

But God's challenge to "remember" the desert was not just for those who experienced it firsthand. God spoke his words to Moses and established practices for his people to obey in order to ensure that his people, from generation to generation, could in a sense return to the desert. He wanted them to remember — to relive its hardships, testing, and intimacy with God — so that it would lead them to live by his every word. So what exactly did God want his people to remember about the exodus and their desert experience?

1. Often the Bible refers to positive aspects of what God accomplishes during "desert" experiences. What do the following verses reveal about God and his people — and what future generations were to remember?

Text	Positive Aspects of Desert Experiences— What Are God's People to Remember?
Deut. 8:2–3	
Ps. 77:11–20	
Ps. 78:52–55	
Ps. 105:37–45	
Jer. 2:1–3	

In what way(s) can remembering these passages and events teach, discipline, and encourage God's people of all times to trust and obey him, depend on his care and protection, and walk in his ways to become who he has called them to be?

In what ways do these passages speak to you regarding your walk with God and the challenges you face in the "deserts" of your life?

2. The Bible does not ignore the hardships of the desert or the struggles the Hebrews faced. As a people who previously had experienced life only in the fertile, well-watered delta of the Nile River, desert life certainly would have been difficult. But part of remembering must include the difficulties, the people's unfaithfulness and complaining, their disobedience, and the dreadful consequences of sin. What do the following passages reveal about God and his people — and what future generations were to remember?

Text	Negative Aspects of Desert Experiences — What Are God's People to Remember?
Deut. 9:7 – 14	
Deut. 32:7 – 15, 20 – 26	
Neh. 9:16 – 21	
Ps. 106:7 – 46	
Ezek. 20:6 – 20	

In what ways does the record of these events — the terrible consequences of sin, God's punishment for sin, and God's faithfulness to forgive and restore his people to his path — serve as a warning and incentive for greater faithfulness to future generations of God's people, including God's people today?

Which warnings are important for you to take to heart as you face "desert" challenges in your life?

FOR GREATER UNDERSTANDING

What Does It Mean to Remember the Desert?

God's prophets frequently pleaded with his people to recall (Hebrew: *zakar*, meaning to recall and act accordingly) their experiences in the desert. In a sense they were challenging God's people to go back to the desert and rejoin his ancient story. They wanted God's people to relive the desert experiences in order to remember God's words and rededicate themselves to the obedient walk he had taught them.

Although Western people are good at mental recall, *experiential* remembering is not the norm for us. To put ourselves back into the ancient biblical story requires significant effort. The closest we normally come to such remembering is our practice of the Communion meal Jesus instructed us to keep. When we participate in Communion, we are not just recalling an experience from long ago. We are, in effect, joining Jesus and his disciples at that meal.

One blessing that people who travel to Bible lands often receive is the feeling that they have joined the ancient story as participants, not simply spectators. Becoming participants by walking in God's ways is a crucial aspect of being part of God's redemptive plan. Whether or not we actually travel to Israel and its desert lands, we are to "remember" as if we had been there.

3. What did Moses command the Israelites to do so that future generations would remember the experiences and lessons of the desert and live by God's every word? (See Deuteronomy 6:4 – 12; 11:18 – 21.)

DID YOU KNOW?

Never in the Israelites' history has God's presence and daily leading been as clear as it was during the desert exodus—at least not until another "word" came out of the desert (John 1:1–10; Luke 4:1–14). In order for his people to remember this intimate time of provision, guidance, and protection, God established a yearly festival called Sukkoth (or the Feast of Tabernacles, Leviticus 23:33–43). For eight days, they lived in temporary shelters and read from the Torah as a way to relive the exodus experience.

4. God intended the Hebrews to become his witnesses to the world of his deity, salvation, power, and holiness (Isaiah 43:10–12).

    a. What did God intend the time in the desert to accomplish in his people so that they could fulfill that calling? (See Exodus 19:4–6; Leviticus 20:7–8, 26; Deuteronomy 7:6–9.)

    b. According to the writers of the Christian text (New Testament), what is the calling of those who follow Jesus? (See 1 Corinthians 1:2; 1 Thessalonians 3:12–13; 1 Peter 2:9.)

    c. How might remembering (*zakar*) Israel's experiences in the desert and remembering all the words of God help us to walk in his ways and fulfill our calling to be his kingdom of priests to our world? What could you do to join in that story yourself?

DID YOU KNOW?

Seeking Refuge in the Desert

Most of us don't think of the desert as being a place of refuge. But when God's ancient people felt overwhelmed by life's suffering or the ungodliness of their culture, they often remembered how God had faithfully provided in the desert. So they went into the desert to seek him.

Elijah, for example, went there (1 Kings 19). Hosea called God's people to return there (Hosea 2:14 – 23). David, chosen by God to become Israel's great king and the "father" of the coming Messiah, spent much time in the desert fleeing from King Saul (i.e., 1 Samuel 24; 26). The Essenes went into the desert as a refuge from their culture so that they could regain the holiness of living by God's every word.

In the solitude of the desert, God's people could hear his voice and words. They could experience his provision and protection. They could derive strength and encouragement from remembering the Israelites' desert experiences. They could focus their effort on obeying God's words and getting to know him in a more intimate way.

5. Why, according to 1 Corinthians 10:1 – 11, must we recall the desert experiences of the exodus?

Which of these warnings and examples address where you are in your walk with God?

What might you understand and learn if you were to study these examples and in a sense relive them as a participant rather than a spectator? How might such an experience change your walk with God?

Reflection

Through the pages of the Bible, the very word of God that has been entrusted to his people (Romans 3:2), we can remember the experiences and the lessons of the exodus. God's Word has the same purpose for his people today that it had for the ancient Hebrews and Jews of Jesus' day — to help us become God's holy people who display him to the world as we live by his every word.

Quoting the words of the prophet Isaiah, Peter reminds us of how essential the Word of God is to our faith:

For you have been born again, not of perishable seed, but of imperishable, through the living and enduring word of God. For, "All men are like grass, and all their glory is like the flowers of the field; the grass withers and the flowers fall, but the word of the Lord stands forever." And this is the word that was preached to you.

1 Peter 1:23–25

What have you learned through this study about the value of God's words (and your obedience to them) in your walk with God?

In what ways have you been inclined to undervalue God's Word?

In what ways does "remembering" the desert experiences help renew your passion for knowing (experiencing) God's words and your commitment to live by them?

Which portions of the Bible have you tended to ignore or view as not being essential to your walk with God, and how might your perspective need to change?

If you, like the Essenes, sought refuge in the "desert" in order to rededicate yourself to walking in God's path, why would the Bible be essential? What books of the Bible do you think would be most essential?

What specific things can you do now to help you know, experience, and learn from God's Word?

Memorize

For everything that was written in the past was written to teach us, so that through endurance and the encouragement of the Scriptures we might have hope.

Romans 15:4

Day Three | Dedicated to the Text

The Very Words of God

> *Praise be to you, O LORD;*
> *teach me your decrees.*
> *With my lips I recount*
> *all the laws that come from your mouth.*
> *I rejoice in following your statutes*
> *as one rejoices in great riches.*
> *I meditate on your precepts*
> *and consider your ways.*
> *I delight in your decrees;*
> *I will not neglect your word.*
>
> *Psalm 119:12 – 16*

Bible Discovery

Understanding the Desert Essenes

The Essenes lived in the wilderness at Qumran as a response to God's command to prepare the way for him in the desert (Isaiah 40:1 – 8). In the solitude of their desert community, they sought to escape the "noise" of a Hellenistic culture, avoid contact with Gentiles and Hellenistic Jews, and remain untainted by the corrupt ruling temple authorities. In the harsh desert environment, they dedicated themselves to intense study of the Word of God (especially the Torah) and living by his every word. They diligently prepared for the apocalyptic age that they believed would soon arrive to purify God's people and install new, godly religious leaders.[1]

1. In order to better understand the Essenes' steadfast commitment to love (obey) God and his Word, we need to realize that religious Jews of the time recognized a connection between the desert and God's words. It was not unusual for them to expect to receive God's words in the desert.

    a. Where did Moses receive God's words, and what was he to do with them? (See Exodus 19:1 – 6; Acts 7:37 – 38.)

b. When God gave his words to his people through Moses, where were they and what were they to do with them? (See Deuteronomy 4:10 – 14; 6:4 – 9; 11:18 – 20.)

c. Where did John the Baptist receive God's words, and how did he respond to them and for what purpose? (See Mark 1:2 – 4; Luke 3:2 – 6.)

d. So if you were a faithful Jew who wanted to obey God and live by his every word, where might you go and how important would it be for you to read, memorize, copy, study, and interpret the Hebrew text?

2. Given this cultural perspective, it is not surprising that the text of Isaiah 40:1 – 8 would "drive" faithful, passionately obedient Jews such as the Essenes into the desert.

a. How much of a commitment would it require to make a straight, level path in the desert — especially in the steep mountains of the Judea Wilderness?

b. How much effort, then, would you expect the Essenes to put into making a way for God by walking in his ways (walking the path of obedience)?

c. Because people walk in God's ways by obeying every word that comes from the mouth of God, what role would the word of God have in preparing the way for the Lord?

DID YOU KNOW?
What Motivated the Essenes?

In addition to scrolls of God's words, the Essenes' writings include studies of books of the Hebrew Bible and documents about the community. In one of those scrolls, the *Manual of Discipline*, we find an explanation of the Essenes' commitment to live in the desert and prepare a path for God:

"And when these [the ones who have become part of the community] exist as a community in Israel … they are to be segregated from the dwelling-place of men of sin [the Jerusalem priesthood] to walk to the desert in order to prepare his path there. As it is written: 'In the desert, prepare the way of … (The Lord)[2], make straight in the desert a roadway for our God.' This is the study of the Torah which he commanded through the hand of Moses … according to what the prophets have revealed through his holy spirit." (*Manual of Discipline, Serekh ha-Yachad*[3] 8:13–16)

DATA FILE

The Community at Qumran

Like many ancient settlements, Qumran was destroyed and rebuilt various times. It was first settled during the Israelite period shortly before the Babylonian captivity (c.a. 600 BC) when it was probably destroyed. It was resettled c.a. 140 BC, during the reign of Hasmonaean king Hyrcanus, but was abandoned after an earthquake (c.a. 31 BC). It became active about the time Jesus was born and remained active until the Roman army destroyed it c.a. AD 68 following the second Jewish revolt.

Qumran's major structures add to our understanding of the community's lifestyle and beliefs. Locate the scriptorium (writing room), *mikveh* (ceremonial or ritual baths, *mikva'ot*, pl.), and refectory (main assembly hall).

Scriptorium. Many archaeologists believe that the Dead Sea Scrolls were written here. Excavation has revealed tables, benches, and inkpots similar to

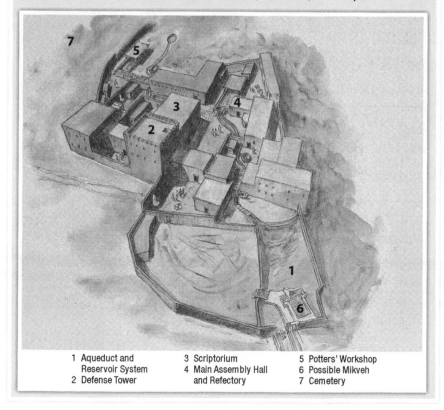

1 Aqueduct and Reservoir System	3 Scriptorium	5 Potters' Workshop
2 Defense Tower	4 Main Assembly Hall and Refectory	6 Possible Mikveh
		7 Cemetery

those used by scribes, as well as basins in which the Essenes could ritualistically wash their hands before and after writing God's sacred name.

Mikveh. Several ceremonial or ritual baths had steps that allowed access to the water. New members were cleansed with water in a type of immersion or baptism that apparently symbolized that they were spiritually clean because of their repentance and God's forgiveness. The Essenes' ritual cleansing likely provided the background for the repentance baptism[4] practiced by John the Baptist. (See Matthew 3:6, 11.)

Refectory. Archaeologists believe the Essenes practiced a communal meal in this main assembly hall in anticipation of the great banquet of the messianic age. A small water channel entering the sloped floor may have allowed the room to be washed before the meal. Nearby, archaeologists have unearthed a kitchen with five fireplaces and a smaller room containing pieces of more than one thousand pottery jars, dishes, plates, and cups.

It is interesting that archaeologists have not found evidence that community members lived in any of the buildings at Qumran. They may have lived in

HUT IN THE JUDEA WILDERNESS

continued on next page . . .

tents or nearby caves. Sparse evidence has been found to prove or disprove either theory. However, Yizhar Hirschfeld of Tel Aviv University recently discovered a settlement of small, stone huts on a steep hillside near En Gedi, about fifteen miles from Qumran. He theorizes (with good support) that a small community like the Essenes, if not actually that group, lived there.

The hut pictured on page 53 at least illustrates the harsh conditions under which the Essenes lived and studied the Scripture. Its rock walls were originally three feet thick and slightly more than four feet high. The floor was beaten clay, and there is a small fire pit in the corner. The roof was probably a tent or a frame covered by palm branches. Although it provided shade, this hut would have been dreadfully hot during the day and cold at night. It illustrates the Essenes' devotion to God and his Word. They willingly gave up comfortable lifestyles in order to live in desert huts such as this because God commanded: "In the desert prepare the way for the Lord" (Isaiah 40:3).

3. Some interpretations, theological concepts, and practices that came out of the Essenes' intense devotion and study of the Hebrew Bible gradually found their way into Jewish culture. So their experience with God's words in the desert helped to shape and prepare first-century Jews to better understand the messages of John the Baptist, Jesus, and the apostles. Consider the following examples:

    a. The Essenes interpreted prophetic Scriptures as being fulfilled by the events of their day, which differed significantly from other religious movements of their time. Why was acceptance, or at least knowledge, of this concept important to God's plan of redemption? (See Matthew 3:1 – 3; Luke 4:14 – 21.)

    b. The Essenes traced the priesthood of the Messiah to Melchizedek, not Aaron. Why is this belief essential to accepting Jesus as the Messiah? (See Luke 1:30 – 33; Hebrews 7:1 – 22.)

    c. The Essenes practiced a ceremonial cleansing using living, free-flowing water. This symbolized their spiritual cleansing that had been accomplished through repentance and forgiveness. How was this similar to the symbolic cleansing the early Christians practiced? (See John 3:22 – 23; Acts 2:36 – 41.)

    d. The Essenes believed their Qumran community was a living sanctuary, more holy than the temple in Jerusalem that they believed had been polluted by a corrupt priesthood. They also viewed themselves as the chosen stones of a new temple in which God's presence was found. How would this concept have helped to prepare the early Christians to understand their identity? (See 1 Corinthians 3:16 – 17; Ephesians 2:19 – 22; 1 Peter 2:4 – 6.)

Reflection

The Essenes at Qumran had a deep commitment to obey God and his Word. They moved to the desert, away from cultural pleasures and pursuits, and dedicated themselves to living by God's words and preparing his way in the desert. They studied God's words and copied books of the Bible. In fact, more copies of the Psalms, many of which David wrote during his time in the Judea Wilderness, have been found among the Dead Sea Scrolls than any other book (thirty-six scrolls).

For a few moments at least, imagine yourself as a participant in the Essenes' desert community and consider what Psalm 119:9 – 16 would mean to you:

> *How can a young man keep his way pure?*
> *By living according to your word.*
> *I seek you with all my heart;*
> *do not let me stray from your commands.*
> *I have hidden your word in my heart*
> *that I might not sin against you.*
> *Praise be to you, O LORD;*
> *teach me your decrees.*
> *With my lips I recount*
> *all the laws that come from your mouth.*
> *I rejoice in following your statutes*
> *as one rejoices in great riches.*
> *I meditate on your precepts*
> *and consider your ways.*
> *I delight in your decrees;*
> *I will not neglect your word.*

In what ways would the psalmist's experience with God's words teach and encourage you as you sought to walk in God's ways?

In what ways would this psalm take you back to the experiences of the Israelites in the desert, where God gave his words (his laws or commands) to his people?

How would being part of a community that had a passion to diligently study and live by God's words help you to know his words and obey them?

Now fast-forward to the present. In what ways does this psalm speak to your life, your passion to know God's words, and your commitment to walk with him?

What specific changes might you need to make in your lifestyle in order to know and delight in the Word of God and faithfully obey his commands in all areas of your life?

Memorize

Do not let this Book of the Law depart from your mouth; meditate on it day and night, so that you may be careful to do everything written in it.

Joshua 1:8

DATA FILE
A Brief History of the Essenes

In about 331 BC, Alexander the Great's armies swept through Israel and continued his campaign to bring Greek culture to every part of the known world.
The Hellenistic culture deeply offended and disturbed devout Jews, but other
Jews were seduced by this secular worldview that glorified the human being
through philosophy, athletics, religion, and the arts.

Initially, Alexander's successors—the Ptolemy family from Egypt—allowed
significant religious freedom for the Jews. During their rule, the Old Testament was translated into Greek, the translation we know as the *Septuagint.*
Later, the Seleucids—Syria's Greek dynasty—brought Israel into their
empire. They aggressively promoted Greek culture, defiled the temple in
Jerusalem with pigs' blood, and dedicated it to their god, Zeus. They banned
the Torah, the Sabbath observance, and circumcision. To violate these bans
meant death. They even sold the position of high priest.

This was too much for the faithful Jews. Led by the Hasmonaean family
(also known as the Maccabees), they revolted and drove out the pagans.
For the first time in nearly five hundred years, the Jews were independent.
The temple was cleansed and rededicated, and worship of Yahweh resumed.
Their great victory became the focus of the Feast of Dedication, known today
as Hanukkah (John 10:22).

The Hasmonaean descendants, however, became thoroughly Hellenistic.
They openly flaunted pagan practices and fought bitterly with followers of
the Torah. This conflict led to the beginning of several sects or "schools"
including the Pharisees, Sadducees, Essenes, Zealots, and Herodians.

The Essenes established a religious movement dedicated to the restoration of
the true worship of God. Their mission was to prepare the way for the Lord,
so they sought to obey his every word and keep their hearts and minds pure
and their practices obedient. They established many practices that set the
stage for Jesus' arrival and teaching. Although small in number, they exerted
significant influence on the religious community of their day.

In 68 AD, the Romans destroyed the Essene community at Qumran. It is possible that the Essenes placed their sacred scrolls in jars and hid them in nearby caves as the Romans approached. Although this community has disappeared from history, its legacy is only now being realized.

Day Four | A Passion for Obedience

The Very Words of God

> *And now, O Israel, what does the LORD your God ask of you but to fear the LORD your God, to walk in all his ways, to love him, to serve the LORD your God with all your heart and with all your soul, and to observe the LORD's commands and decrees that I am giving you today for your own good?*
>
> **Deuteronomy 10:12–13**

Bible Discovery

No Sacrifice Is Too Great

The Essenes' passion to walk in God's ways (path) by obeying his every word was exemplary. They willingly sacrificed the comforts of life and the pleasures of culture in order to live in the desert wilderness and focus their full attention on knowing and obeying God's words. But they had a problem in the desert. In order to fulfill their interpretation of God's commands, they needed "living" water — fresh, free-flowing water from a spring, stream, or rain — to use in their purification rituals.

How would they obtain such water in the desert? It wouldn't be easy! But they were committed to doing whatever was required — to raise up every valley and level every mountain — to prepare a way for God (Isaiah 40:3 – 4). So they undertook an ambitious construction project. Using only hand tools, they created catch basins, built dams, chiseled a tunnel, and made an aqueduct on a steep, rocky mountainside to carry runoff from occasional floods into their settlement. The evidence of their hard labor still testifies to their intense, sacrificial devotion to obey God. Consider the words of God that inspired such passionate obedience among the Essenes.

1. The "way of the Lord" is obedience to his commands, and the Essenes studied the Hebrew Scriptures in order to know how to obey God's commands completely — to walk (Hebrew: *halak*, "walk," "live," "obey") in God's "way" or "path" (Hebrew: *derekh*). Take some time to read and meditate on the following passages of Scripture about God and obeying his words. As you "take in" God's words, how much passion and love for walking in God's ways do they inspire in you?

Text	My Insights, My Response
Deut. 5:28–33	
Deut. 10:12–13	
Deut. 13:4	
Deut. 26:16–17	
Deut. 30:15–16	
Ps. 25:4–5, 8–10	
Hos. 14:9	

2. God desires more from his people than intellectually *knowing* the right path. The practical application of the way or path of God — the text of the Hebrew Bible — is to walk obediently in God's way. This kind of faith is not only a set of

beliefs and doctrines; it is God's words lived out in daily life. What kind of effort does God desire his people to expend in obeying his words? (See Deuteronomy 10:12; Psalm 15:1 – 4; 119:30 – 32; Isaiah 57:14 – 15.)

What impact do you think that these and similar passages of Scripture had on the Essenes' commitment to work diligently and put extreme effort into all aspects of their walk with God?

If you had been an Essene — tired, sweaty, dirty, thirsty, hot from laboring in the desert's burning sun — which of these passages would have been going through your mind as you chiseled rock or carried stones to build a dam in order to bring living water into your community?

DATA FILE

"Living" Water in the Desert

The Essenes followed a holy God and were committed to obeying all of his commands. They recognized that participating in sin would make them spiritually unclean, so they went into the desert in order to focus on living the righteous life God desired. They also followed the Torah commands for ritual cleansing of the body following contact with something unclean (body fluid, disease, contact with a corpse, etc.).

continued on next page . . .

MIKVEH **AT QUMRAN**

In their community, they regularly practiced a ritual bath—a type of immersion or baptism—that symbolized the purification of heart and soul God provided as a result of a person's repentance and commitment to obey his words. The ritual cleansing was done in a *mikveh* (*mikva'ot*, pl.). According to the Essenes' interpretation of the Hebrew Bible, the water needed to be "living" water—fresh, free-flowing water from a spring, stream, or rain.

There is no "living" water near Qumran. The Essenes could have transported water by donkey or cart from the springs of Ein Feshka several miles away, but it would not have been "living" water. Instead of compromising their beliefs and practices, the Essenes exerted great effort to capture flood waters in the mountains above their settlement and direct it into their community.

Using only hand tools, the Essenes created catch basins and a dam in a steep, rocky mountainside where runoff from occasional floods cascaded over a cliff. They tunneled through more than one hundred feet of dolomite (hard limestone) to bring that water to the cliff's edge, then directed it through more than a thousand feet of plaster-coated channels and aqueducts until it reached their settlement and ran into reservoirs and *midva'ot*.

Just imagine how difficult it was to bring "living" water into Qumran. Imagine the time spent laboring under the burning, relentless sun. Imagine the hours spent on hands and knees to chip out a tunnel. Imagine the fatigue of moving rocks by hand to build dams and channels. And the Essenes did all of it because they lived by a passionate commitment to obey God—to prepare his path in the desert—with all their heart, soul, and strength.

THE HAND-CHISELED WATER TUNNEL AND AQUEDUCT CARRIED "LIVING" WATER FROM THE MOUNTAINS ABOVE TO THE SETTLEMENT AT QUMRAN.

Reflection

It is important to remember that the Essenes did not make this passionate commitment to earn salvation. Rather, like their Hebrew
ancestors at Mount Sinai, obedience was a response to God's deliverance. Jesus will teach the same lesson (John 14:15). As you reflect on
what the Essenes sacrificed in order to fulfill their passionate commitment to obey every word from the mouth of God, please allow
me (Ray) to share some of the impact their example has had on me.

It is hard to describe how harsh the conditions are in the Judea
Wilderness. The scorching sun, the intense heat, the dust, and the
scorpions make this a hostile place. A part of me is amazed that the
Essenes left behind the comfort and luxury of a Hellenistic culture
in order to endure the hardships of the desert so that they could live
the righteous, obedient life God desires. Their level of devotion to
God and to his words inspires me.

For a long time I struggled with the Essenes' devotion to the Bible in
comparison to mine. I prayed often for God to give me their fire and
level of devotion. Then a Jewish friend told me I had it backward!
"Read Jeremiah 20:9," he said. I read it, and I understood.

I had wanted the fire in me to bring discipline and power to my
reading and study of the Bible, but the fire is in the Bible! The fire is
in God's words. So I began to read and study much more. I may not
yet have the level of devotion of the Essenes, but the fire is burning.

Do you, like the Essenes, have "God's fire in your bones"?

How much do you want that fire?

What are you willing to do to "fan the flames"?

As you devote yourself to reading and studying God's Word, when have you felt the "fire" igniting in your heart?

What was it like, and what did it compel you to do?

In what ways has the Essenes' extreme obedience and devotion to God and his words, as demonstrated in part by their industrious water project, influenced your commitment to knowing and obeying the Word of God in all areas of life?

How willing are you to sacrifice your relatively comfortable lifestyle in order to carry out the mission — in order to build the "tunnel" — God has for you?

What is the "tunnel" that God may be calling you to build as an act of faithful obedience to him?

What personal cost are you willing to bear in order to build the "tunnel" that will impact your culture for God?

Day Five | Live the Text and Wait for God's Glory

The Very Words of God

> *When the time had fully come, God sent his Son.*
>
> *Galatians 4:4*

Bible Discovery

The Revelation of God's Glory Comes

The Essenes took to heart God's command in Isaiah 40 and went into the desert. They separated themselves from the prevailing Hellenistic culture in order to know and worship God. Their devotion led to new ways of living the text and preparing God's way by obeying his words in all aspects of life. Knowing that God had promised to come and walk among his people, they diligently worked to prepare the "way," and eagerly awaited the day when his glory would be revealed. And just as God had promised, his glory was revealed at the coming of Jesus the Messiah!

1. In light of what you have learned through this session of studies, reread Isaiah 40:1 – 11 and consider the Essenes' example of heartfelt commitment to "live the text."

   a. Scholars believe this reference to Jerusalem's suffering to be Assyria's destruction of Israel (722 BC) or the Babylonian captivity (586 BC), which resulted from the unwillingness of God's people to "walk his path." What insight into God's character might the Essenes have gained from this text, and how might it have inspired their devotion to walk in God's ways?

b. In the ancient world, it was customary to provide a special road for the coming of a king. How enormous a job is it to make a road fit for a king? What kind of commitment and effort does it require — especially if the path is to be prepared in the desert? How might that explain the effort the Essenes expended to obey God's words completely?

c. Why do you think the Essenes believed that the way to prepare God's highway was to study God's Word and passionately obey it?

d. The amazing promise in Isaiah's prophecy is that when the path was prepared — by repentance and rededication to righteous living — the presence of the Lord would appear! What does the Essenes' willingness to cast aside everything and devote themselves to knowing and living the text reveal about the depth of their desire to be with their God?

2. In what ways had the "glory of the LORD" been revealed to God's people in the past, and what did it represent? (See Exodus 24:15 – 17; 25:22; 40:34 – 35; Leviticus 9:23 – 24; 2 Chronicles 5:13 – 14; 7:1 – 3.)

3. As the Essenes lived the text and walked the path of righ-
    teous obedience to prepare the way for God, they antici-
    pated the coming of his glory. In fact, it is likely that they
    expected God himself to come and live among his people.

    a. What occurred in Bethlehem, a village at the west-
        ern edge of the Judea Wilderness, and by the Jordan
        River just five miles away from Qumran? (See Matthew
        1:18 – 23; 2:1; 3:1 – 3, 13 – 17.)

    b. What might be the relationship between the Essenes
        who were committed to walk in God's righteousness
        and the location where Jesus first appeared among his
        people?

    c. After the way was prepared, what did the sovereign
        Lord, the Messiah, do once he appeared among his
        people? Is this what the Essenes might have expected?
        Why or why not? (See Isaiah 40:10 – 11; John 10:11 – 16;
        Hebrews 13:20 – 21.)

THINK ABOUT IT

Prepare the Way By Living It!

There are few flat and open places in the Judea Wilderness, so it would take an enormous effort to make a way—a highway—here. The height of the mountains, the depth of the valleys, and the harsh terrain and desert environment made preparing a path for God in the Judea Wilderness a monumental task.

THIS IS A TYPICAL DESERT *DEREKH* (PATH) IN THE JUDEA WILDERNESS NEAR QUMRAN. NOTE THE RUGGED MOUNTAINS AND DEEP VALLEY.

Clearly God's challenge to his ancient people—and to his people today—is to expend superhuman effort in our desire to walk in God's path. Yet because the Christian text emphasizes salvation by grace (Acts 15:11; Ephesians 2:8–9) for which we praise God, the call for his people to be passionately committed to walking his path by obeying him is sometimes muted. All too often, we study the path—define it, proof-text it, enshrine it in creeds and statements of faith, teach it, memorize it, and even separate from other people over it—but put little effort into *living* that path.

continued on next page . . .

Jesus and his disciples knew that genuine faith demands more than knowing about the path. It demands *halakah*—obediently walking in God's way, practically applying the path of God in daily life (Matthew 7:21; John 14:15; James 2:14–26). God is not satisfied when we simply know the truth. After all, even the evil one knows it! God desires us to live the truth in our daily walk—to walk as Jesus walked (1 John 2:3–6).

4. The oldest Greek manuscripts of the Christian Bible (New Testament) often reflect the idea of preparing the way of the Lord, as the Essenes did, by "walking" (obeying) his word on the "path" or "road" of daily life. How do the following passages impress on you the importance of walking in the way of God? (See Matthew 7:13 – 14; John 8:12; Acts 18:24 – 26; 24:14 – 16; 1 John 1:5 – 7; 2:6.)

Reflection

The Essenes' commitment to the Scriptures is astounding. Rarely in the history of God's people have they left comfortable lives to live in difficult conditions in order to copy, study, interpret, and seek to obey the Word of God and prepare the way for his coming. The Essenes did not interpret all of Scripture correctly, but their devotion to God's ways and words should be an example to all of us.

The prophet Isaiah, whose message drove the Essenes to labor diligently in the desert preparing the path for God, also has a compelling message for those of us who follow Jesus today. Isaiah 2:1 – 3 foretells that during the last days people from all nations will go to God's mountain, saying, "He will teach us his ways, so that we may walk in his paths." Just as the Essenes had a role in preparing the way for the Messiah because they obediently lived for God, those of us who have a personal relationship with God through Jesus must be fully committed to walking God's path so that we can fulfill our role in his unfolding story of redemption.

> We are called to prepare the way so that people who are living in spiritual darkness will be drawn to God and his Word. Is this a compelling motivation for you? Why or why not?

> How carefully are you seeking to obey God in every area of your life each day?

> How passionately do you devote yourself to in-depth study of God's Word? Are you willing to stay up late or get up early just to learn the words of God?

> How hard will you work to keep your heart and mind pure before God and your lifestyle obedient to his commands?

You have a path to prepare! God wants all the world to know him, and you are his witness. So go, live by his words and walk in his ways.

Memorize

This is what the LORD says: "Stand at the crossroads and look; ask for the ancient paths, ask where the good way is, and walk in it, and you will find rest for your souls."

Jeremiah 6:16

THE WAY OF JOHN THE BAPTIST

John the "Baptist" (or John "the Immerser"[1] as he was likely known by the people of his day), is frequently portrayed in early Christian art and iconography. In these early depictions, he is always pointing — sometimes at the figure of Jesus, sometimes at nothing in particular. For example, on Charles Bridge in Prague in the Czech Republic, a large statue sculpted in 1857 by Josef Max depicts John holding a cross with one arm and, with the other arm extended, pointing at no one in particular.

John's life's mission was to point, as he eloquently put it, to the greater one who would come after him — the one "the thongs of whose sandals I am not worthy to untie" (Luke 3:16). Today, millennia after his martyrdom, the legacy of John's mission continues. He is still remembered for pointing beyond himself to the coming Messiah who came and will return to earth again.

Although John passionately focused his life on the Messiah rather than on himself, this desert prophet has played an influential role in the history of God's people, particularly during his own time. In fact, ancient historical sources tell us more about John than they do about Jesus! Josephus, a first-century Jewish historian, wrote an extensive account of John's life and work, especially his death at the hands of Herod Antipas. In addition, the Dead Sea Scrolls have provided valuable insights into the religious and cultural context of first-century Jewish life — the movement of which the Essenes were a part, the reasons devout Jews sought him in the desert, the anticipation of the imminent arrival of the Messianic King, and the practice of the baptism of repentance — that help us to better understand why John's message had such a powerful impact on his world.

John's movement became so popular that it initially may have spread earlier and more widely than the community of Jesus-followers, although both faith communities eventually blended together. On reaching Ephesus nearly twenty-five years after Jesus' ascension, for example, the apostle Paul met people who belonged to the movement of John the Baptist (Acts 18:24 – 19:7).

John's life was completely focused on pointing toward the Messiah who was to come and on preparing the people to receive him. We have much to learn from his understanding of how to prepare for the arrival of the Messiah. His message of repentance, obedience, and concern for justice and the needy is remarkably relevant to our chaotic times. His intense and courageous commitment to his mission and message, even when it required him to speak an unpopular message to authorities in power, and his refusal to compromise even to the point of martyrdom, reflect qualities rarely exhibited today among Jesus' community in the Western world.

So let's delve into the life and mission of this devoted prophet of God. Let's explore the relationship and purpose Jesus and John shared. Let's focus on John's message of repentance and hope. That message was so important to him that he literally died in order to live by God's Word and point the way to the coming Messiah.

Opening Thoughts (3 minutes)

The Very Words of God

John

> He will be great in the sight of the Lord. He is never to take wine or other fermented drink, and he will be filled with the Holy Spirit even from birth. Many of the people of Israel will he bring back to the Lord their God. And he will go on before the Lord, in the spirit and power of Elijah, to turn the hearts of the fathers to their children and the disobedient to the wisdom of the righteous — to make ready a people prepared for the Lord.

Luke 1:15 – 17

Think About It

Consider people you have met who are totally and completely passionate about something — perhaps their job; a political, cultural, or spiritual cause; their children; a hobby. Which words would you use to describe such people — their commitment to devote time and resources to their passion and their focus in pursuing activities that support it?

How would you describe what is required to passionately pursue something? How would you describe the commitment required for a follower of Jesus to live a life of passionate commitment to God, his Word, and his kingdom?

DVD Notes (29 minutes)

John the Baptist:

Strengthened in spirit in the desert

Coming in the spirit and power of Elijah

Sent to call for repentance and to prepare the way

Was John an Essene?

Imprisoned at Machaerus

Our challenge to love, live, and die the text

DVD Discussion (6 minutes)

1. In what ways did learning that God often takes his people
    into the desert in order to strengthen their spirits and pre-
    pare them to accomplish his work give you greater insight
    into how God works in the lives of his people — and how he
    may be working in your life?

    He tests us to see so we what is in our hearts

baptize means to wash - get wet

2. What did you learn about the ways in which John "the Immerser" demonstrated in character, word, and action (even by where he ministered and what he wore) the spirit and power of Elijah? *he had the passion -*

Read 1 King - 17

In what ways did this "Eastern" manner of creating multiple visual, geographic, tangible, and mental images help to make his message more powerful?

3. What was John's message, and in what ways did it prepare the way for Jesus? *Repent as the Kingdom of God is near.*

4. The messages sent between John and Jesus while John was in prison were rooted in the text of the Hebrew Bible. How well did they have to know the text in order to communicate as they did? *Very well*

Is your knowledge of the Bible such that you and others in your faith community would be able to communicate in this manner? *No*

To what extent do you think a deep knowledge of and obedience to God's words are vitally important to followers of Jesus today?

5.   What did you feel as you learned about the events of John's imprisonment and execution at Machaerus?

What is the impact of John's legacy on your walk with God?

Small Group Bible Discovery and Discussion (17 minutes)

Born to Be the "Elijah to Come"

Among God's people, Elijah earned the reputation of being an intense, obedient servant of God who put every ounce of strength he had into God's service. So, to call someone an "Elijah" would be to recognize that person as being totally committed to God. John, the "Elijah to come" of the Gospels, gave every ounce of strength he had to serving God and pointing the way toward Jesus. Of course, John's accomplishments were made possible by the power of God. Yet, as is often the case, when God chose John, he chose a "partner" who would serve obediently with *all* of his might.

1. What amazing news did the angel Gabriel bring to Zechariah concerning the character and life purpose of his future son, John? (See Luke 1:11 – 17.)

Based on the angel's message and the reputation of Elijah, what kind of person would Zechariah and his wife, Elizabeth, have expected their son to be? (See 1 Kings 18:16 – 46.)

What does Luke 1:80 reveal about John and his preparation for fulfilling his mission?

THINK ABOUT IT
A Day in the Life of Elijah

Elijah was intensely committed and passionately obedient to God. No one worked with such fervor and stamina or risked greater personal harm to purge idolatry from God's people. Consider what this prophet did — in a single day — to call God's people back to obedience to God (1 Kings 18:16 – 46):

- Climbed Mount Carmel, about a 2,200-foot, five-plus-mile climb. The distance is approximate because we don't know the exact location to which he climbed, but we know he could see the Mediterranean Sea and that he climbed down to the Kishon River.
- Challenged the Israelites to "get off the fence" and choose between their God and Baal.
- Harassed the Baal priests.

continued on next page . . .

- Built an altar of twelve large stones on which he placed a bull he had slaughtered.
- Prayed passionately for fire from heaven.
- Descended to the Kishon River with 900 hundred captured Baal and Asherah priests—a 2,200-foot, five-plus-mile descent—and had them all killed.
- Once again made the 2,200-foot, five-plus-mile climb up Mount Carmel, prayed for rain, made the 2,200-foot, five-plus-mile descent and ran ahead of King Ahab's chariot to the palace at Jezreel (a distance of at least fifteen miles)!

John grew up knowing the Elijah story. Imagine how he must have prepared himself knowing that he was to follow Elijah's example.

2. What was John's message? (See Mark 1:4; John 1:26–34.)

Baptism of repentence

Do you think he believed that he was the messenger preparing for the Lord's coming? Why or why not?

3. In very Jewish ways, John invited his audience to consider the possibility that he was the voice in the wilderness predicted by Isaiah — that he was the messenger who would come in the spirit of Elijah to prepare the way of the Lord (Isaiah 40:1 – 11; Malachi 3:1; 4:1 – 6).

   a. In what visible way did John link himself to Elijah, and what did his audience understand John to be communicating to them? (See 2 Kings 1:7 – 8; Matthew 3:4; Mark 1:1 – 8.)

   dressed like him — did baptizing where Elijah did

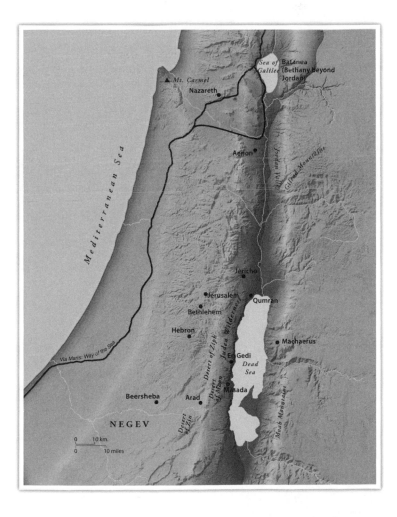

b. John also linked himself to Elijah by carrying out his mission in three distinct "Elijah places" that biblically literate Jews would recognize. On the map on page 81, locate the three places where John baptized: Judea Wilderness by the Jordan, Aenon near Salim, and Bethany beyond the Jordan (Batanea). Then read why each of these places was a significant "Elijah place" and what John did in each area.

Location	What Elijah Did Here	What John Did Here
Batanea (Bethany beyond the Jordan)	1 Kings 17:1–6 (Kerith is believed to be Wadi Yarmuk):	John 1:24–34:
Aenon near Salim, also known as Abel Meholah	1 Kings 19:15–16, 19–21:	John 3:22–30:
Judea Wilderness by the Jordan	2 Kings 2:7–15:	Matthew 3:1, 13; 4:1:

c. How many Christians today know the Bible well enough to recognize the verbal, visual, and geographic allusions that John used to portray himself (and Jesus) as the fulfillment of the ancient Hebrew prophecies?

d. What might we be missing out on in our relationship with God and in our ability to fulfill the mission to which he has called us if we don't know the Word of God well?

DATA FILE
The Three "Elijah Places" Where John Baptized

Wilderness of Judea. John baptized Jesus here, along the Jordan River between where it enters the Dead Sea and fifteen miles north of it. Immediately after Jesus' baptism, he entered the desert, which adds credibility to this location. Recent excavations in Jordan east of Jericho have uncovered a large Christian complex from the early Byzantine period that includes many baptismal pools, at least five churches, and guesthouses along a spring-fed stream that ran into the Jordan River. The early church apparently believed this was the location of Jesus' baptism.

Aenon near Salim. This is on the west side of the Jordan where John's disciples expressed concern about the popularity of Jesus baptizing people. John pointed out that he was not the Messiah, therefore it was appropriate for his role to lessen while that of Jesus became greater.

Batanea (Bethany beyond the Jordan). This location has been debated since early church times. There was a place that later (fourth century AD) was named Bethany beyond the Jordan east of Jericho, but it seems likely that Batanea was a region east-northeast of the Sea of Galilee.[2] Several factors make this likely: (1) some Jewish sources designate this region as Bethany; (2) Essene activity occurred in this area; (3) Jesus apparently came here after opposition in Jerusalem — a logical decision if Batanea is Bethany beyond the Jordan, which would have been outside Herod Antipas' territory; (4) John 10:40 calls it a "place" and not a village; and (5) Jesus first contacted some of his disciples in Bethany beyond the Jordan, then went to nearby Galilee.

Faith Lesson (4 minutes)

In first-century Israel, rabbis (teachers) often used words or phrases that their audience would recognize from the Hebrew text in order to add power and understanding to their teaching. When Jesus said, "From the days of John the Baptist until now, the kingdom of heaven has been forcefully advancing, and forceful men lay hold of it" (Matthew 11:12), the Greek word translated "forcefully," *biazo*, no doubt brought Micah 2:12 – 13 to the minds of Jesus' audience. This passage likened exiled Jews to a flock of God's faithful sheep waiting in a pen for God to open the way and free them. Micah prophesied that one person would "break open" the way so that, led by their King, the flock would "break through" the gate.

The Hebrew root word *pratz*, translated as "break," implies an explosive breaking out. Jesus was presenting John the Baptist as the one who broke open the way so that he — the Messiah — would lead the faithful flock out into the world. Jesus not only confirmed that John was the prophet and messenger that Isaiah said would come (Matthew 11:9 – 13), he also affirmed and complimented John's passionate and explosive devotion to his mission. Jesus said that John prepared the way in the spirit and power of Elijah so that the healing *shalom* of God's kingdom could break out into our sin-broken world!

1. In John's life, we see a hero of faith whose passion and intensity set an example for us to follow. The Messiah may not have come exactly as John expected, yet God used John as he had Moses, David, and Elijah to break open the path for Jesus.

   a. What do you think John the Baptist, who was facing death in Herod's isolated fortress, felt when his disciples relayed Jesus' divine affirmation to him?

b. How great is your desire to serve Jesus with the passion and spirit that John did and to hear him affirm your life's labor?

2. Jesus challenged his disciples to continue his ministry of bringing *shalom* to the world. To break out and lay hold of the kingdom of God requires not only speaking the teachings of Jesus, but living them.

    a. In what ways do you consider it your mission to walk as Jesus walked (1 John 2:6) and model his compassion, love, forgiveness, and care for hurting people?

    b. Which specific things are you committed to doing every day, every week, and every month in order to walk as Jesus walked?

    c. Which things do you have a passion to do but are not presently doing, and what is your plan to make them a part of your life?

3. What hinders you from having a walk with Jesus that breaks open the way to defeat evil in the world?

Closing (1 minute)

Read together Matthew 11:11 – 15: "I tell you the truth: Among those born of women there has not risen anyone greater than John the Baptist; yet he who is least in the kingdom of heaven is greater than he. From the days of John the Baptist until now, the kingdom of heaven has been forcefully advancing, and forceful men lay hold of it. For all the Prophets and the Law prophesied until John. And if you are willing to accept it, he is the Elijah who was to come. He who has ears, let him hear."

Pray for ears to hear the words of Jesus and a passionate, committed heart to obey them. Praise God for the legacy of those, including John the Baptist, who have willingly sacrificed their lives in order to advance the kingdom of heaven.

Memorize

> *I tell you the truth: Among those born of women there has not risen anyone greater than John the Baptist; yet he who is least in the kingdom of heaven is greater than he. From the days of John the Baptist until now, the kingdom of heaven has been forcefully advancing, and forceful men lay hold of it. For all the Prophets and the Law prophesied until John. And if you are willing to accept it, he is the Elijah who was to come. He who has ears, let him hear.*
>
> *Matthew 11:11 – 15*

Learning to Walk in the Way of the Lord

In-Depth Personal Study Sessions

Day One | Why Did John Live in the Desert?

The Very Words of God

> *And the child grew and became strong in spirit; and he lived in the desert until he appeared publicly to Israel.*
>
> *Luke 1:80*

Bible Discovery

Becoming Strong in Spirit in the Desert

The Judea Wilderness, which was close to the well-watered, fertile fields and populated cities of the Judea Mountains, had long been a place of sanctuary for God's people. It is where David found refuge and drew close to God while hiding from King Saul. The Essenes lived there to separate themselves from the corruption of the prevailing culture and to prepare a way for the coming of the Lord. And it is where John the Baptist lived and fulfilled his calling.

In the big picture, God's people have gone into the desert — just as they did during the exodus from Egypt — to learn to hear the words of God and, by living in obedience to them, to become his holy people who are equipped to fulfill the mission God has given them. Like many before him, John the Baptist went into the desert where God strengthened his spirit and raised him up to be a godly prophet who powerfully prepared the way for the coming of the Lord.

1. The Scripture tells us that as John the Baptist grew up in the desert, he became "strong in spirit" (Luke 1:80), which is a Hebrew way of saying he became passionate and strong in his heart and mind concerning his God-given mission. In contrast, the Hebrew word that describes the heart and spirit of the Hebrew slaves in Egypt (translated as

"discouragement" in Exodus 6:9) literally means "weakness of spirit" or "crushed spirit."

a. Where did God lead his people whom he had set free from bondage in Egypt so that they would develop a strong and willing spirit? (See Exodus 15:22; 16:1 – 3; 17:1; 24:3 – 7; Deuteronomy 8:1 – 5.)

b. What was essential to God's training of his people in the desert during the time of Moses? (See Deuteronomy 4:1 – 2, 5 – 10; 11:18 – 23; Acts 7:37 – 38.)

c. What did God give John in the desert to strengthen and prepare him for his mission? (See Luke 3:2.)

2. In addition to being the desert region closest to the populated areas of the Promised Land, the Judea Wilderness had special significance in the hearts of God's faithful people. Consider some of the reasons John may have been drawn into this particular desert to grow strong in spirit.

a. The Judea Wilderness was God's provision and refuge. How did God provide for David when he was hiding from Saul here, and what did he learn about God's provision, his ways, and his word? (See Psalm 18:1 – 6, 16 – 19, 25 – 36.)

b. The Judea Wilderness was where God removed the
    sins of his people. On Yom Kippur, the Day of Atone-
    ment, the High Priest would take the scapegoat out of
    the temple to the top of the Mount of Olives, look back
    toward the temple (west) where God's presence lived,
    and symbolically place the sins of the people on the head
    of the goat. The goat would then be taken east into the
    desert (the Judea Wilderness) and pushed off a cliff to its
    death. Thus the desert where John the Baptist prepared
    the way and baptized also symbolized God's removal and
    forgiveness of the sins of his people "as far as east is from
    the west." How do you think the location of John's cry
    to "confess" and "repent" intensified his message to his
    audience? (See Leviticus 16:20 – 22; Psalm 103:6 – 12; Jer-
    emiah 31:33 – 34, 37.)

c. The Judea Wilderness was also a reminder of God's
    future restoration of *shalom* to his world. The prophet
    Ezekiel used the side-by-side contrast of the fertile fields
    of the Judea Mountains against the barren wilderness
    to point to God's future restoration. As you read Ezekiel
    47:1 – 12, envision the landscape of the Judea Wilder-
    ness actually changing as the stream of water flows from
    God's presence in the temple in Jerusalem. What miracu-
    lous changes take place, and could they ever occur apart
    from God's power? What does this say to you about the
    loving heart of God and his delight in bringing restora-
    tion and healing to his people?

IMAGINE FLOWING WATER, FRUITFUL TREES, AND ABUNDANT LIFE THRIVING IN THIS DESERT!

d. The Judea Wilderness also reminded God's people of his promise to be their helper in times of trouble. In that wilderness, David had written psalms about God's faithfulness. According to Jewish tradition, worshipers who came from the north and east for festivals in Jerusalem began to sing these psalms while climbing the steep, dangerous road from Jericho in the Rift Valley up through the Judea Wilderness into the city. Read one of these Psalms, Psalm 121, and imagine thousands of people reciting it as they labored to walk uphill in scorching desert heat and anticipated being in the presence of God. In what ways does this psalm reiterate the lesson God's people learned in the deserts of the exodus — that they could depend on their God to lovingly care and provide for them, even in vast, dreadful, waterless desert lands?

e. Most important, the Judea Wilderness reminded God's people that they hear his words most clearly in the desert. God gave his words in the desert, and what does he want his people always to remember about them? (See Deuteronomy 4:10; 8:2 – 3; Isaiah 40:8; Acts 7:38.)

DATA FILE
Was John an Essene?

Since the discovery of the Dead Sea Scrolls and subsequent insights into the practices of Essenes, scholars have discussed whether John was connected to that community.[3] Did he live at Qumran? Did he see the Dead Sea Scrolls? Write any of them? These questions have been asked because of the remarkable similarities between the Essenes and John's teaching and practices that are highlighted below:

John the Baptist	The Essenes
Came from family of priests (Luke 1:5)	Many were priests who rejected the validity of the corrupt temple authorities
Lived in the Judea Wilderness (Luke 1:80)	Qumran was in the Judea Wilderness
Was called to "prepare the way for the Lord" (Isaiah 40:1 – 5)	Lived in the wilderness to prepare the way for the Lord
Baptized as a sign of repentance and inner cleansing (Mark 1:4 – 5)	Practiced ritual cleansing in water as a sign of the soul's cleansing
Proclaimed that the One to come would baptize with the Holy Spirit (Mark 1:7 – 8)	Believed God would pour out his Spirit like water to cleanse perverse hearts
Was not accepted by many people (Matt. 21:32)	Complained that people ignored their teachings
Didn't participate in the normal lifestyle of his people (Mark 1:6)	Lived an ascetic existence; prepared their own food

continued on next page . . .

John the Baptist	The Essenes
His disciples fasted and recited prayers (Mark 2:18; Luke 11:1)	Fasted; had specific prayers
Was in conflict with Jerusalem authorities (Matt. 3:7–10)	Wanted to create a new temple and religious practices

These similarities do not make John an Essene. There is historical evidence that those in the Essene movement took in young children to train them in obedience to God.[4] So at a young age, John may have been shaped by Essene teaching. However, if John had been an Essene, the Dead Sea Scrolls, Bible, or other ancient texts do not mention it. (Josephus did write about a later "John the Essene," a military commander during the first revolt.)[5]

John's mission to live in the desert and call God's people to repentance and holy living in order to prepare the way for the coming Messiah, although similar, differed from that of the Essenes. The Essenes did not evangelize and John called all of Israel—including tax collectors and soldiers—to repentance and obedience to God's Word (Luke 3:10–14).[6] The Qumran community was a separatist group, and John called everyone to repentance and baptism, then sent them back into culture (and apparently to the temple's rituals and ceremonies) to live in righteous obedience to God.

Reflection

Today it is vital for us, as it was for John and followers of Jesus who came after him, to remember why God took his people into the desert. We may never go into a desert physically, yet God uses other types of "desert" — financial loss, loneliness, natural disaster, loss of loved ones, or other unwanted changes and difficulties — to challenge us to depend on and obey God and his Word and to thereby grow strong in spirit.

Although the desert is God's training ground, we can perish there if we don't have help. When you face desert times in life, where and how do you tend to seek help?

Is it the kind of help that will strengthen your spirit? How do you know?

In what specific ways has God helped you by his words and physical provision during "desert" times?

In what ways has his provision strengthened you in your walk with him and enabled you to go out and fulfill his calling in your life?

In what ways does remembering what God did for you in the "desert" help you in your daily life and provide a refuge when the path you walk is particularly difficult?

Day Two | John's Divine Mission

The Very Words of God

"Do not be afraid, Zechariah; your prayer has been heard. Your wife Elizabeth will bear you a son, and you are to give him the name John. He will be a joy and delight to you, and many will rejoice because of his birth, for he will be great in the sight of the Lord. He is never to take wine or other fermented drink, and he will be filled with the Holy Spirit even from birth ... he will go on before the Lord, in the spirit and power

of Elijah, to turn the hearts of the fathers to their children and the disobedient to the wisdom of the righteous — to make ready a people prepared for the Lord."

Luke 1:13 – 15, 17

Bible Discovery

Born for God's Purpose

The stage was set for "preparing the way for the Lord." The era of Roman "peace" brought roads throughout the Roman empire, enabling the good news of the gospel to be spread across the entire region. The Romans made Greek the common language of most of the empire (with the exception of Judea, where most people spoke Hebrew and Aramaic).

But Rome's "peace" came at a price. In Judea, ordinary Jews who passionately obeyed the Torah suffered under corrupt, Hellenistic chief priests and the violent brutality of Roman occupation. They longed for the peace their Messiah would bring. To faithful Jews who understood the prophets, it appeared that everything was ready ... except the coming of the "Elijah" who would precede the Messiah.

Then one day a righteous and ordinary priest named Zechariah made his way toward the Holy Place of the temple — probably for the first and only time in his life. Chosen by lot from hundreds of priests assembled in the Hall of Hewn Stone, he would place incense on the altar symbolizing the prayers of God's people. In the east, the sun was rising over the Mount of Olives. The shofar had already blown from the temple's pinnacle. As other priests prepared for the morning sacrifice, Zechariah entered the marble temple. Soon there would be news of "Elijah's" coming to prepare the way.

1. How did Luke describe Zechariah and his wife, Elizabeth, and why do you think he needed to emphasize that Zechariah was a "righteous" priest? (See Luke 1:5 – 7.)

   Are Zechariah and Elizabeth the kind of people God chooses as "partners" in fulfilling his plan of redemption? Why or why not?

   Do you think they thought God would use them in a great, miraculous way? Why or why not?

2. What amazing thing occurred when Zechariah was alone in the Holy Place, and how did he respond? (See Luke 1:10 – 22.)

DATA FILE

The Offering of Incense

During the first century, more than twenty thousand priests served in the temple worship.[7] Since the time of David, they had been divided into twenty-four "courses" or "brigades" (1 Chronicles 24:3, 6 – 19), and each course served for one week twice a year. It is unlikely that a priest chosen for the high honor of offering incense would carry out that responsibility again.

continued on next page . . .

Accompanied by two other priests, the chosen priest would enter the semi-darkness of the Holy Place. The seven-branched menorah burned to their left side; to their right the table held the twelve loaves of bread. In the center, in front of the veil, stood the golden altar of incense. One priest removed remains of the previous day's offering, then left backward in respect for the Lord's presence. The second priest spread live coals removed from the altar of sacrifice onto the altar of incense and also backed out.

Hearing the prayers of people who lay prostrate outside pleading for God's mercy and blessing that they would know fully only when the Messiah came, the chosen priest stood alone. Holding the golden censor in his hand, he poured incense onto the altar and added his prayers to those of the faithful. Then he, too, backed out and stood on the temple steps overlooking the praying people. He joined all the other priests in raising their hands and chanting together the blessing God had given Aaron to place on the people: "The LORD bless you and keep you ... make his face shine upon you ... and give you peace" (Numbers 6:24–26).

Just imagine what it would have been like to receive a message from an angel in this setting—especially a message about the one who would prepare the way for the long-awaited Messiah! Imagine the curiosity and speculation of the worshipers regarding what was taking Zechariah so long to perform his duties inside the Holy Place.

3. When Zechariah first heard the angel's message, he questioned it and the angel made him unable to speak (Luke 1:18 – 22).

    a. When God allowed Zechariah to speak again, how did he respond? (See Luke 1:57 – 64, 67 – 79.)

    b. How did Zechariah and Elizabeth's neighbors respond, and what did they recognize when these things happened? (See Luke 1:65 – 66.)

    c. Throughout human history, the kingdom of God comes when God demonstrates his power in a mighty way and his people acknowledge, bless, and praise him and seek to obey him with all their heart, soul, and strength. (The story of the crossing of the Red Sea in Exodus 14:13 – 15:18 would be an example.) As you see the story of John the Baptist unfolding in Luke 1:5 – 15 and 57 – 79, what hints do you see that the kingdom of God is about to be revealed?

DID YOU KNOW?

The Lord Is Gracious

The name God's angel assigned to the child, "John" (Hebrew: *Jehochanan*) means "The Lord is gracious," which represents an answer to Zechariah's prayer for a son (Luke 1:13). As a priest, Zechariah also prayed for God's mercy and blessing for his people. God answered that prayer as well by sending John to prepare the way for the coming mercy and blessing God would provide to all people through the long-awaited Messiah.

4. The angel Gabriel's message was specific about who John would be and what he was to accomplish. (See Luke 1:13 - 17.)

   a. What would be his character before God and people (vv. 14 - 15)?

   b. What requirement did God place on his life (v. 15)?

   c. What were the five parts to John's mission that would help to prepare for the Messiah (vv. 16 - 17)?

5. John believed that once the way was prepared, the glory of the Lord — his awesome presence — would appear to gently lead his flock (Isaiah 40:10 - 11). But the task God had given him of making ready "a people prepared for the Lord" (Luke 1:17) would not be easy. Consider the faithful commitment and hard work John put into fulfilling his purpose.

a. In keeping with the angel Gabriel's instructions, what lifelong vow did John take? (See Luke 1:15.)

DID YOU KNOW?

The Nazirite Vow

People who took the Nazirite vow did so as an indication of total devotion to God's service for a specific length of time—even, as in John's case, for a lifetime! The vow, described in Numbers 6:1–21, indicated a "separation to the LORD" and involved a commitment never to drink wine or other fermented drink, never to eat anything from a grapevine, and not to cut one's hair. Jews of Jesus' day understood that such a vow indicated a person's passionate dedication to carry out a mission for God with one's whole being.

b. Where did John go and how did he live in order to fulfill his God-given purpose? Which words would you use to describe John's commitment to fulfill his mission? (See Mark 1:4 – 6.)

c. What difficult message did John come to preach, and what did it cost him? (See Matthew 3:1 - 6; Mark 6:17 - 28; Luke 3:19 - 20.)

THE JUDEA WILDERNESS, WHERE JOHN FULFILLED HIS MISSION TO PREPARE THE WAY FOR THE GLORY OF THE LORD

6. Knowing that John would fulfill his mission for God, what high commendation did the angel of God bestow on him (Luke 1:14 – 17), and which other biblical characters have received such high praise from God? (See Deuteronomy 34:10 – 12; Mark 9:2 – 7; Hebrews 11:1 – 16.)

Reflection

John was born to fulfill a specific mission — to prepare the path for the coming Messiah — and he undertook that task with amazing passion. Today, God also commands those who follow Jesus to be active in his service. Many of us, however, tend to assume that God will bring about what he desires regardless of our faithfulness in completing the work he gives us. Apathy, self-gratification, and laziness never were words to describe John the Baptist. He knew that if he remained faithful and diligent to the work God gave him to do that the kingdom of God would come!

In what ways might you be underestimating the significance of your commitment to obey God and give sacrificially of yourself in order to accomplish the work he has set before you?

How do you want to change that?

What makes someone "great in the sight of the Lord," and is this a goal for which we should strive? Why or why not?

By taking the Nazirite vow, how serious a commitment did John make to pursue God's purpose with all his heart, soul, and strength?

In a land where the basic diet comprised figs, grapes, olives, and grains, how easy was that vow to keep?

How might such a vow keep a person focused on God and dependent on his divine sustenance to accomplish his work?

What are you willing to do without and leave behind in order to pursue and accomplish the mission God has for you?

Do you think Jesus' followers today have a mission similar to that of John the Baptist to prepare people for the coming of the Lord? Why or why not?

Memorize

Therefore, since we are surrounded by such a great cloud of witnesses, let us throw off everything that hinders and the sin that so easily entangles, and let us run with perseverance the race marked out for us. Let us fix our eyes on Jesus, the author and perfecter of our faith, who for the joy set before him endured the cross, scorning its shame, and sat down at the right hand of the throne of God. Consider him who endured such opposition from sinful men, so that you will not grow weary and lose heart.

Hebrews 12:1 – 3

Day Three | John and Jesus

The Very Words of God

> *The next day John saw Jesus coming toward him and said, "Look, the Lamb of God, who takes away the sin of the world! This is the one I meant when I said, 'A man who comes after me has surpassed me because he was before me.' I myself did not know him, but the reason I came baptizing with water was that he might be revealed to Israel." Then John gave this testimony: "I saw the Spirit come down from heaven as a dove and remain on him. I would not have known him, except that the one who sent me to baptize with water told me, 'The man on whom you see the Spirit come down and remain is he who will baptize with the Holy Spirit.' I have seen and I testify that this is the Son of God."*

John 1:29–34

Bible Discovery

John the Baptist and Jesus: Two Lives Connect for the Glory of God

John the Baptist and Jesus shared a divinely ordained bond — one the preparer of the way, the other the glory of the Lord. As they lived in obedience to God's words and fulfilled his purpose for their lives, their paths crossed. Their interaction and statements indicate great respect and honor for each other — and an even greater respect for obeying and fulfilling God's words. People from all over Judea came to see them — some, of course, out of curiosity, but many more in response to their call for repentance and righteous living. Together, John and Jesus made a tremendous impact on their world.

1. The mothers of John the Baptist and Jesus were relatives who each became pregnant (although in very different ways) by God's design and power, in order to fulfill his plan of redemption. John would be born about six months before Jesus, but before their births their mothers spent three months together. What indication of their unborn sons' future relationship did these women experience, and what

do you think it meant to them? (See Luke 1:26 – 37, 39 – 45, 56.)

2. The Bible reveals little about the lives of John and Jesus during their growing-up years. By the time they each began their public ministry, which probably would have been at about age thirty, they apparently did not know each other. From what common place did they begin to proclaim God's message?

    a. John (See Matthew 3:1 – 2; Luke 1:80.)

    b. Jesus (See Matthew 3:13 – 4:1; 4:12 – 17; Mark 1:9 – 15.)

3. What message did John and Jesus preach? (See Matthew 3:2; 4:17; 9:35; Mark 1:14 – 15; Luke 3:3.)

4. Who did some people believe Jesus to be, and who did some people believe John to be? (See Matthew 16:13 – 14; Luke 3:15; 9:7 – 9.) What does this indicate about both men's intense devotion to God and to their respective missions?

5. Even among God's people who seek to serve him, it is not
    uncommon for disagreements, criticism, or jealousy to
    adversely affect their relationships and their ministry. Cer-
    tainly such opportunities existed in the lives of Jesus and
    John, but what driving passion and commitment motivated
    both men, and how was it reflected in their attitudes and
    behavior toward one another? Consider the following:

    a. *The baptism of Jesus.* (See Matthew 3:13 – 17.) How do we
        know that John was surprised by Jesus' coming to him
        for baptism? How did Jesus convince John that it was the
        right thing to do? What amazing revelation did God make
        after the baptism?

    b. *The concern that some of John's disciples had regard-
        ing Jesus' popularity among the people.* (See John
        3:22 – 30.) What did John say that revealed his knowl-
        edge of who Jesus was and how he (John) felt toward
        him? What do you think enabled John to respond to
        their changing status among the people with joy rather
        than jealousy?

    c. *The great commendation that Jesus gave concerning
        John after John had been imprisoned by Herod.* (See
        Malachi 3:1; Matthew 11:7 – 14; 17:10 – 13.) What did
        Jesus affirm about John's identity, and what honor did he
        bestow on John because of his (John's) commitment to
        obey the words of God at all costs?

d. *Where Jesus baptized after John the Baptist died.* (See John 10:40 – 42.) Why do you think Jesus went back to the place John had baptized? In what ways did his presence there affirm and honor John's role in preparing the way for Jesus? What impact did John's testimony continue to have on the hearts of people?

e. *What Jesus' disciples asked him to do that they had seen John do with his disciples.* (See Luke 11:1 – 4.) How did Jesus respond? Imagine the impact of the prayer Jesus taught in response to John's practice of teaching his disciples to pray. What impact does it still have on people?

FOR GREATER UNDERSTANDING
A Difference in Expectations

While John was imprisoned by Herod, he sent his disciples to ask Jesus if he was "the one who was to come" (Matthew 11:1 – 6). It is not likely that John was doubting Jesus' identity. After all, John had baptized Jesus. He had seen heaven open and the Spirit descend in bodily form like a dove. He had heard God's voice declare that Jesus was his beloved Son with whom he was very pleased. But John was confused. The Messiah had come, yet John was sitting in Herod's prison, a place from which very few left alive.

Like many faithful Jews of his day, John apparently understood from the prophecies of Malachi that the appearance of the messenger who would prepare the way and the judgment day of the Lord would occur simultaneously. So his expectation of imminent, divine judgment against all forms of evil didn't seem to fit with a Messiah who focused on bringing redemptive healing to the sinful and broken rather than crushing the forces of evil. Jesus apparently had a different timeline. Yes, the great and terrible day of the Lord when he would complete his task of judgment would come (Matthew 25:31–46; John 5:27, 30), but first the Messiah would come as the Lamb of God to demonstrate the ways of the kingdom of heaven.

6. Despite the similarities of their message, there were differences in John and Jesus' expectations of what would happen once the way had been prepared and the glory of the Lord appeared.

   a. In contrast to what John had interpreted the Messiah's coming to be like (Matthew 3:7 – 12; Luke 3:15 – 18), what was the focus of Jesus' ministry now that the "road" was built up and obstacles removed? (See Isaiah 57:13 – 19; Zechariah 9:9 – 12; Matthew 11:5.)

   b. How might passages such as Isaiah 13:6 – 11 and Malachi 4:1 – 5 have influenced John, who knew that he was fulfilling the role of the "Elijah to come" to usher in the coming of the Lord?

   c. Might Jesus' audience have understood the "trees-without-fruit" parable (Luke 13:6 – 9) as a correction of John's expectations? (See also Luke 3:8 – 9.) Why or why not?

    d. In what ways did John's message achieve its purpose even though the day of Messiah's coming was not exactly what John had expected? (See Luke 3:16; 7:29.)

7. How did Jesus respond when Herod executed John? (See Matthew 14:6–23.)

Reflection

John the Baptist and Jesus had a special relationship, one clearly "made in heaven" even before they were born. They both passionately obeyed God and his word; they both labored diligently to deliver their message ... and people responded! Luke wrote, "All the people, even the tax collectors, when they heard Jesus' words, acknowledged that God's way was right, because they had been baptized by John" (Luke 7:29).

What kind of a statement would you want an observer to make about the testimony of your life?

How much of a privilege would you consider it to be if you were the "preparer," the one who pointed the way so that another person could see or hear God and acknowledge that his ways are right?

Elijah (as well as John, the "Elijah to come") was passionate, fiery, determined, and committed to obey and serve God. Yet James 5:17 reveals that Elijah "was a man just like us," which means in the original Greek expression that he had the same attitudes and feelings we do. Do you think it is possible for you to have the same passionate zeal to obey God that Elijah and John the Baptist had? Why or why not?

What may be hindering you from having the commitment and passion to prepare the way for Jesus' next coming?

How might John's faithful example encourage you to be God's partner in the next chapter of his unfolding story of redemption?

Memorize

Then John gave this testimony: "I saw the Spirit come down from heaven as a dove and remain on him. I would not have known him, except that the one who sent me to baptize with water told me, 'The man on whom you see the Spirit come down and remain is he who will baptize with the Holy Spirit.' I have seen and I testify that this is the Son of God."

John 1:32 – 34

Day Four | John's Message of Repentance

The Very Words of God

> *In those days John the Baptist came, preaching in the Desert of Judea and saying, "Repent, for the kingdom of heaven is near." ... People went out to him from Jerusalem and all Judea and the whole region of the Jordan. Confessing their sins, they were baptized by him in the Jordan River.*
>
> *Matthew 3:1–2, 5–6*

Bible Discovery

Repent! For the Kingdom of Heaven Is Near

When the time was right, God gave John a message to proclaim. In true biblical fashion, John came out of the desert — where God had taken the Israelites to learn to live by his every word — proclaiming a message that resonated from one end of the land to the other. The message itself was simple: "Repent, for the kingdom of heaven is near."

Because the way of the Lord was the way of obedience, repentance was necessary to prepare the way and a people to receive the Messiah. Repentance was necessary for the kingdom of God to come — and when he came, the Messiah would demonstrate how to live the life of that kingdom. John's message of repentance is no less relevant today. Our world desperately needs the fresh anointing of God's presence. It will come as his people once again prepare the way for his presence by their repentance and obedient demonstration of the life of his kingdom.

1. Both John and Jesus proclaimed a powerful message of repentance. John came with a fiery passion to call people who lived in an ungodly culture to repentance and obedience in order to prepare the way for the Messiah. Jesus came as the Messiah to demonstrate the ways of the kingdom of God. Note how these purposes are evident in their teaching:

    a.   What was the emphasis of Jesus' message? (See Matthew 7:18 – 23; Mark 1:14 – 15; Luke 13:2 – 8.)

    b.   What was the emphasis of John's message? (See Matthew 3:1 – 8; Luke 3:8 – 9.)

DID YOU KNOW?
The Hebrew Meaning of Repentance

The Hebrew word commonly translated "repentance," *teshuvah*, literally means "to return," as when someone walking in one direction suddenly turns and walks in exactly the opposite direction. To a Jewish way of thinking, one's remorse for sin, although important, is not nearly as important as taking that first step away from sin. In contrast, the Greek word translated "repentance" in the earliest Christian (New Testament) texts emphasizes the change of mind and heart that lies behind a change of path.

John's teaching, rooted in the Hebrew text, emphasizes the change of path that must occur because of remorse or change of attitude. Being sorry for sin but choosing to continue in it is not repentance. God forgives his children when they sincerely ask, but the sincerity of their request is demonstrated by their change of path. The healing freedom and restoration that God brings to a repentant person is experienced in the effort made to walk obediently on God's path.

WHAT IS THE KINGDOM OF GOD?

The kingdom of God can be described as God reigning over the lives of people who enthrone him as their King. The purpose of the kingdom is to defeat the power of evil and restore *shalom* to God's creation. God commands his people—from the ancient Hebrews to today's Christians—to bring his reign to the world so that all people will acknowledge him as Lord.

Jewish scholars believe that God's kingdom was first seen during the exodus:

- The kingdom broke into the chaos caused by sin when God, using the plagues that Pharaoh's magicians attributed to the "finger of God," acted with miraculous power to release the Hebrews from Egyptian bondage (Exodus 8:19). The kingdom appears as God acts with great power.
- The Hebrews responded to God's deliverance at the Red Sea by calling him Lord and dancing before him as they acknowledged his reign over all things (Exodus 15:18). The kingdom appears as people respond and acknowledge him as Lord.
- God brought the Hebrews to Mount Sinai so that they could enthrone him as King in their lives by learning to obey him (Exodus 19:4–6).[8] The kingdom appears as people extend his reign by obeying his will for their lives.

The kingdom of God is central to the message of the New Testament as well. The "good news of the kingdom" is that when Jesus the Messiah—God's Son—arrived, so did the kingdom. Jesus' miracles, especially his redemptive death on the cross, was the "finger of God" breaking into the chaos of sin.

When people hear the good news that the kingdom is among them, some repent and call him Lord. Forgiven and freed from sin, they seek to obey God so that he reigns in their lives. Their desire is expressed in the prayer Jesus taught: "Your kingdom come, your will be done" (Matthew 6:10). Until the day that every knee will bow and every tongue will confess that Jesus is Lord (Philippians 2:10–11), the kingdom of God lives wherever God reigns—in the lives and hearts of his people who do the will of God by obeying his every word.

2. Calling God's people to righteousness in order to prepare the way of the Lord was not simply correcting their theology but recalling them to the mission God had given their ancestors: to live such good lives that all the world would come to know him.

    a. How does the Hebrew Bible describe a righteous life? (See Exodus 22:21 – 22; 23:1 – 9; Leviticus 19:33 – 37; 23:22; Deuteronomy 10:16 – 20; 15:7 – 11; 24:19 – 21.)

    b. Why does God command such a life? (See Deuteronomy 10:17 – 18.)

3. Through John's passionate "repentance proclamation," the way for the coming of the Lord was prepared. Read Luke 3:7 – 18, noticing how people responded to John's message and what they wanted to know about how to live the kingdom life.

    a. How did John answer the crowd when they asked what they needed to do to produce the fruit of repentance?

    b. What is significant about tax collectors and soldiers asking John what they needed to do to produce the fruit of repentance?

c. When the people who heard John's message went back to their families and communities, what do you think may have happened that advanced the kingdom of God? Why?

d. Why do you think some of them thought John was the Christ? In what ways do you think John's obedience produced evidence of the kingdom of God?

FOR GREATER UNDERSTANDING

The Kingdom of God vs. the Kingdom of Heaven

The first-century Jewish community hesitated to say the sacred name of God lest they "take it in vain." So they used synonyms for the name such as "Mighty One" or "Lord." Jesus also used the word "heaven" as a designation for God. Thus the kingdom of God became known as the kingdom of heaven.

The same accounts of Jesus' teaching in Matthew and Luke appear to use different terminology to describe the kingdom, but these titles are synonymous. Matthew was probably a Jew and is believed to have written to a Jewish-Christian audience. He frequently recorded Jesus as speaking of the kingdom of heaven. Luke, on the other hand, was probably a Gentile who wrote to a Gentile-Christian audience. He freely used the designation kingdom of God.

4. Despite the power of his message, not everyone responded positively to John's cry for repentance and obedience to the way of the Lord.

    a. Which groups of people who came to John to be baptized felt they had no need to produce the fruit of righteousness, and what was John's warning to them? (See Matthew 3:7 – 12.)

    b. To which group of people did Jesus tell a parable about a tax collector and Pharisee, and what was his message about our need to repent? (See Luke 18:9 – 14.)

    c. Which agricultural metaphor did John use to describe the coming judgment for those who would not repent and produce the fruit of righteousness, and how might they have responded? (See Matthew 3:7 – 12.)

DATA FILE

Threshing in First-Century Israel

Like the prophets before him, John used threshing as a metaphor to portray God's judgment (Amos 1:3; Isaiah 41:15 – 16). Dating back to Bible times, this threshing floor of exposed limestone bedrock near Bethlehem is larger than most. At harvest time, the stalks of grain were cut, tied into bundles,

continued on next page . . .

and left to dry. Then the stalks were spread out on the hard floor to be threshed. At this location, an ox or donkey pulled a sled around and around over the grain, separating kernels from stalks. On a windy day, farmers used winnowing forks to toss the grain into the air. The chaff blew away; the heavier grain fell to the ground to be gathered.

DATA FILE

Religious Parties of Jesus' Time

The Sadducees claimed to be descendants of Zadok, the high priest during the reigns of David and Solomon. According to Josephus (*Antiquities* 6, 10, 13), they were the party of the wealthy upper class. They accepted only the written Torah, not the rest of the Hebrew Bible, as authoritative and rejected the scriptural interpretations of the Pharisees and Jesus.

The Sadducees denied the existence of angels and demons and did not believe in a resurrection or immortality of the soul (Acts 23:8). They treated ordinary people harshly, especially the poor and needy. Their strict, literal interpretation of Torah prevented many people from becoming part of the religious practices God had ordained to restore broken people to himself.

The Pharisees began as a separate sect within Judaism and first appeared as a powerful political party in opposition to the Sadducees during the time of the Maccabees (166–163 BC). Godly "ordinary" people considered Pharisees to be successors to Moses and therefore guardians of the Jewish faith. In contrast to the increasingly pagan Greco-Roman-Hellenistic lifestyle of many Jews, particularly temple leaders, the Pharisees' interpretations of Torah focused on holiness, righteousness, and purity—not in an effort to obtain salvation, but in response to God's redemption. Many of Jesus' interpretations of the Hebrew Bible are similar or even identical to those of the Pharisees.

Pharisees established many synagogues and schools, and their rabbis made disciples who also passionately walked with God. Despite their unfortunate reputation as hypocritical legalists—hypocrisy that Jesus and the Pharisees themselves strongly criticized—many (if not most) Pharisees passionately followed God. They helped to preserve the legacy of the Scripture and thus prepared for the coming Messiah.

The Zealots violently opposed Rome and the idolatrous Hellenism of pagan Greeks and Romans. They believed the kingdom of God/heaven would come as a result of violent opposition on the part of God's people. Originally the term "zealot" described anyone who was "zealous" for the honor and sanctity of the Lord and the purity of the priesthood and the temple services. They used the Hebrew Bible in ways similar to the Pharisees. Probably after Jesus' time, the Zealots became a more formal movement.

5.   Both John and Jesus practiced repentance baptism by immersion in water as a symbol of the work of repentance God was accomplishing in the hearts of his people. What kind of baptism did they say would follow, and what do you think that baptism represented? (See Matthew 3:11 – 12; Luke 3:16 – 17; John 1:33 – 34; 3:5; Acts 2:1 – 4.)

DATA FILE

The Baptism Practiced by John

The baptism John practiced in the Jordan River or springs running into it was an outward sign of repentance. Before entering the "living" water, the individual had to have a clean heart, which occurs only by God's forgiveness based on the person's penitence and commitment to obedience. This practice was similar to the baptism of the Essenes that required they "not enter the water ... unless they turn from their wickedness."[9]

John apparently exhorted people to repent—to turn from disobedience and commit to a righteous walk—before being baptized. That is why he demanded the fruit of repentance—righteous living—before they were immersed (Luke 3:7 – 8). Thus Jesus, who was pure— *without sin*—before he came to John, was the perfect candidate for John's immersion. Jesus' baptism by John symbolized his perfect purity as the Messiah.

Reflection

Perhaps the secularization of the Christian community that we see today is due to our failure to recognize how sin interferes with God's desire to work through his people. Only a righteous, fruitful community of people can bear the fruit of repentance and display the kingdom of God to the world. Repeatedly Jesus said that those who love him will obey his teachings (John 14:15, 21, 23 – 24). We cannot obey his teachings if we don't deal with our disobedience. We cannot display the kingdom of God if we don't "produce fruit in keeping with repentance."

In what ways do you acknowledge your disobedience to God's teachings and turn toward the right path in order to prepare the way for the presence of God's kingdom to be seen in your life?

What disobedience in your life currently interferes with producing fruit and being an instrument of God's kingdom?

In the spirit of true repentance, the tax collectors and soldiers (Luke 3:12 – 14) asked John, "What should we do?" Why is it important for you to ask this question of God, and when was the last time you asked it?

In what way(s) does your faith community practice some form of public repentance and rededication to obedience in order to prepare the way for the presence of God to flow powerfully through that community?

Can God be actively enthroned in the life of an individual or a community of faith in which the poor are not fed, the stranger is not cared for, and other people in need are not helped? Why or why not?

What specific things are you doing (or will you commit to doing) to obediently reveal the presence of God's kingdom in your community by responding to these needs as Jesus would?

Day Five | John Lived and Died the Text

The Very Words of God

> *And with many other words John exhorted the people and preached the good news to them. But when John rebuked Herod the tetrarch because of Herodias, his brother's wife, and all the other evil things he had done, Herod added this to them all: He locked John up in prison.*
>
> *Luke 3:18 – 20*

Bible Discovery

Always Faithful to the Word

Moses and Elijah, great prophets of God who spent significant time in the desert, never saw the completion of the God-given work they had pursued. Moses died on Mount Nebo before the Israelites entered the Promised Land (Deuteronomy 34:1 – 8). Elijah, who passionately fought to see righteousness restored among God's people, was taken up to heaven before that hope was fulfilled. And so it was for John. He prepared the way for the Messiah's coming, but was imprisoned and martyred before he saw the fruit of his preaching. In fact, John's absolute commitment to obey God's word and fulfill his God-given mission of calling people to repentance led to his death.

1. During the exodus, God gave his words to his people so that they would obey his commands and learn how to live righteous lives. He also gave commands for the rulers of his people to help the people remain faithful to God. What were those commands, and which of them do we know Herod Antipas violated? (See Exodus 20:1 – 17; Leviticus 18:16; Deuteronomy 17:14 – 20; Luke 3:19 – 20.) Why would Antipas' Jewish subjects have rejected his legitimacy as king if he violated Torah?

    Why do you think John — a desert preacher and prophet whose mission was to prepare the way for the Messiah — rebuked Herod Antipas for his divorce and subsequent marriage to Herodias, as well as for his other evil actions?

    To what extent do you think John's personal commitment to a life of obedience to God's words compelled him to speak out?

    Would you think this was an issue worth dying for? Why or why not?

What does John's willingness to die for this reveal about his fervent passion to obey God and preach the message of repentance God had given to him?

DATA FILE

The World of Herod Antipas

In 37 BC Herod the Great became king of Judea. A visionary and ingenious builder, he oversaw legendary construction projects that included a spectacular palace complex and the marble and gold temple in Jerusalem; fortresses that included the Herodion, Masada, and Machaerus (where John the Baptizer apparently was beheaded); a palace in Jericho; and the largest man-made harbor in the world at Caesarea. But his cruelty overshadows his other accomplishments.

To remain in power among God-fearing Jews, he relied on the might of Rome and support from the Hellenistic temple authorities. He cruelly suppressed any resistance, real or imagined. He killed potential political rivals as well as some of his wives and children. When faced with the threat of Jesus' coming, Herod even killed the infant sons of Bethlehem (Matthew 2:16).

Hated even by his family, Herod eventually died a dreadful, agonizing death in his palace in Jericho. Roman Emperor Caesar Augustus endorsed his will that split up his realm between three sons. Archelaus received the best territory of Judea, Samaria, and Idumaea (in the southern Negev region). Herod Philip would rule the largely Gentile but poor area north and east of the Sea of Galilee. Herod Antipas received Galilee and Perea—the most religious regions where there was ongoing unrest.

Supported by Pharisees and Herodians (a largely upper-class secular group), Herod Antipas brought prosperity and uneasy peace to Galilee and Perea. But his pro-Roman policies, combined with pagan decadence, caused tension. When Antipas divorced his wife and married Herodias, his brother Philip's

THE DIVIDED TERRITORIES OF HEROD THE GREAT'S REALM

wife, while Philip was still alive, he incurred the bitter opposition of the religious Jews.

Antipas imprisoned and eventually beheaded John the Baptist because he criticized his unlawful marriage to Herodias. John's execution haunted Antipas for the rest of his life. It also brought opposition from another Jewish rabbi: Jesus. When Jesus was brought to Antipas before his crucifixion, Jesus refused even to speak to him.

NOTE: To learn more about the Herod dynasty, refer to *Faith Lessons vol. 3: Life and Ministry of the Messiah*, Sessions 1 and 2; and *Faith Lessons vol. 4: Death and Resurrection of the Messiah*, Session 4.

2. The story of John the Baptist, Herod Antipas, and Jesus is
   fascinating. Read Matthew 14:1 – 12; Mark 6:14 – 29; and Luke
   3:19 – 20; 9:1 – 2, 7 – 9, taking careful note of the details in
   the motivation and interaction between the people involved.

   a. What picture do the Gospel writers paint of Herod Antipas?

   b. Although Herod was the ruler, who had real power in this
      story and why? In what ways was that power evident?

   c. Why do you think Herod was so intrigued by John and
      his message?

   d. What personal struggle did Herod have about executing
      John, and what impact did John's death have on him for
      the remainder of his life?

DID YOU KNOW?

Herod the Great, king of the Jews when John the Baptist and Jesus were
born, was a descendant of Esau (Genesis 25:23 – 26). Jesus was a descendant of Jacob. It was no surprise to religious Jews who knew the Hebrew
Bible that conflict occurred when the prophecies about Jacob and Esau came
true (Numbers 24:17 – 19; Amos 9:11 – 12; Obadiah 1:18).

3. What provided an opportunity for Herodias to have John killed, and what does the disciples' action afterward reveal about John's relationship with Jesus? (See Matthew 14:3 – 12; Mark 6:17 – 28.)

4. In what ways does the story of John the Baptist — the Elijah to come — and Herod Antipas remind you of another king, wife, and faithful prophet? (See 1 Kings 16:29 – 17:1; 18:16 – 18, 41 – 19:2.)

DATA FILE

Machaerus, Where John the Baptist Died

First-century historian Josephus wrote a fascinating report of John's execution by Herod Antipas in about 30 AD at the mountain fortress of Machaerus.[10] Josephus described John as a good man who urged fellow Jews to live obediently and practice justice and piety. His account includes the story of Herod's divorce from the daughter of Aretas, king of Petra, and his marriage to Herodias, his brother's wife. In response, Aretas went to war against Herod and soundly defeated him, which led first-century Jews to believe that God caused Herod's defeat as punishment for his execution of John the Baptist.

Originally built by Hasmonaean King Alexander Jannai (103 – 76 BC) to defend against desert tribes to the east and south, Machaerus is five miles east of the Dead Sea and thirty miles from Jerusalem. Rebuilt and strengthened by Herod the Great (37 – 4 BC), the walled fortress included a magnificent palace stocked with provisions to withstand a long siege. According to Roman historian Pliny, Machaerus was the most important fortress in Judea after Jerusalem. It was abandoned after the first Jewish revolt in 66 AD.

continued on next page . . .

MACHAERUS

The upper city on top of the mountain measured 360 feet by 200 feet east to west. It had a wall six feet thick with eighty-foot-tall towers at the corners. Inside the wall, the palace was divided into two main wings by a paved hallway. The eastern wing had a paved courtyard covering a large cistern and included hot baths. The western wing had a peristyle garden (open court surrounded by columns and a roof) and a triclineum (a banquet hall where guests reclined as they dined). A lower city existed on the mountain's steep north slope, and an aqueduct supplied water to cisterns dug into the mountainside.

Reflection

John died because of his absolute faithfulness to God's Word. Whereas many of us might be tempted to compromise or be silent, John continued to proclaim God's words and it cost him his life. In Matthew 11:11, Jesus praised John for being the greatest man born to that point in history! Yet Jesus added that the least of *us* in the kingdom is even greater than John!

John risked his life to criticize Herod Antipas for what some people today might view as a "personal" issue. What does this reveal about John's absolute devotion to the Word of God?

What is your desire to live faithfully before God, and what encouragement for your life do you find in John's faithful obedience to the Word of God?

In what way(s) does our unwillingness to obey *all* of God's words — not just the words we feel like obeying — compromise the authority of God's Word and our ability to impact our neighbors, friends, faith communities, and culture?

Do you think John's words could have led people to repent of their sins and turn to God if he had not lived a righteous life? Why or why not?

Do you know anyone who lives out the biblical text with passion and consistency? If yes, how might you build a relationship with that person that strengthens each of you in your devotion to God and his words and your passion to live a righteous life? If not, how might you find such a person?

In Greek, James 5:17 literally says that we have the same "attitudes and feelings" as Elijah — the one John was like! To what extent are you living in light of your Elijah-like commitment to demonstrate your love for Jesus by obeying every word of God?

Memorize

If you love me, you will obey what I command.... Whoever has my commands and obeys them, he is the one who loves me. He who loves me will be loved by my Father, and I too will love him and show myself to him.

John 14:15, 21

INTO THE DESERT TO BE TESTED

God's story began when he demonstrated his power over chaos at creation. Merely by the power of his words, he set boundaries for chaos and created a beautiful, harmonious universe. No sooner had this great triumph been accomplished than chaos, in the form of the crafty serpent, reared its ugly head. With the simple question, "Did God really say . . . ?" the evil one tempted the people God had created to rebel against his word. In so doing, the harmony (the Bible calls it *shalom*) of God's creation was destroyed and chaos returned.

This was not the end of God's story, however. God began the process of restoring *shalom* to his broken creation. The experiences of God's people during the exodus are not only the first chapter of this story, they are a paradigm for the ongoing story of restoration that continues to the present time. Whenever God demonstrates his power over chaos in a great and mighty way — whenever the *shalom* of his kingdom moves forward — temptation or testing will soon follow.

When God demonstrated his mighty power over chaos to deliver the Hebrew slaves from Egypt, he took them into the desert (chaos, to their way of thinking) to test what was in their hearts so that he would know whether or not they would keep his commands (Deuteronomy 8:2 – 3). In the land of chaos, God spoke his words and through difficult experiences began to mold and shape his people. As they practiced their fledgling faith during the journey to Mount Sinai, they began to learn what it meant to live by every word that comes from the mouth of God.

At Sinai God spoke, giving his chosen people the greatest mission any people have ever received. As his treasured possession (Exodus 19:5 - 6), they were to be a holy nation — his kingdom of priests — who would display him to the world. They needed not only to profess him as Lord as they had on the shores of the Red Sea, they needed to enthrone him as their King by faithfully obeying his every word. Then God's kingdom would advance, and *shalom* would begin to be restored to his creation.

Although the Israelites often chose chaos over *shalom* during their ensuing forty years of testing in the desert, God continued to teach and shape them. They successfully prepared a new generation that emerged from the desert as a people who obeyed and trusted God with all their heart, soul, and strength. They were imperfect, to be sure, but they enthroned God as their King and embraced the mission he had given them to fulfill in the Promised Land.

When Jesus was baptized, God had demonstrated that his power was at work. The heavens separated, the Spirit descended on Jesus like a dove, and the voice from heaven declared, "You are my Son, whom I love; with you I am well pleased" (Luke 3:21 - 22). Temptation or testing would certainly follow, and the Bible says that the Spirit then led Jesus into the desert. There, the evil one sought every opportunity to sabotage God's plan by drawing the Messiah away from his intended purpose of restoring God's *shalom* to all things through his death and resurrection.

Jesus' desert experience "echoed" the testing of the Hebrews in the Sinai Desert. By using the exact Torah text that described the tests the Hebrews experienced in the desert more than a thousand years earlier, Jesus thwarted the evil one. His faithfulness during these temptations demonstrated that God was, indeed, enthroned in his life as Lord and King. His steadfast commitment to live by every word that comes from the mouth of God rather than to pursue his own purposes (or those of the evil one) affirmed that he embraced God's mission without reservation. After being tempted, Jesus emerged from the desert to proclaim that the kingdom of heaven (God) was at hand (Mark 1:12 - 15).

Jesus' temptations — and the lessons they provide — help us to understand the nature of God, Jesus his Son, and the evil one. They provide significant insights into temptations we face. Because the temptations occurred in a desert setting, they provide a link between the Hebrews, Jesus, and our calling to be a "royal priesthood" (1 Peter 2:9), to be God's witnesses to a broken world. All who follow Jesus will face testing, "desert" times, and attacks by the evil one who understands that the kingdom of God born in the desert will cause his demise. So let us "walk" with the Messiah into the desert to be molded and shaped as God's people.

Opening Thoughts (3 minutes)

The Very Words of God

> Therefore, since we have a great high priest who has gone through the heavens, Jesus the Son of God, let us hold firmly to the faith we profess. For we do not have a high priest who is unable to sympathize with our weaknesses, but we have one who has been tempted in every way, just as we are — yet was without sin.
>
> **Hebrews 4:14 – 15**

Think About It

It is exciting and inspiring to see God work in powerful ways. Think, for example, of the excitement the Hebrews felt when God delivered them at the Red Sea. Immediately afterward, they were "pumped" and felt ready to tackle anything! Their God reigned! But were they really who they thought they were at that moment? Did they have the knowledge, ability, and commitment to follow through and obediently accomplish the task God had given to them? How might a test or two help them to discover what they were lacking so that they could complete their "education" in God's ways?

In what ways might we need testing to reveal our flaws and weaknesses so that we can learn to walk in God's ways?

DVD Notes (30 minutes)

Jesus and his relationship with the desert

Jesus is baptized; the testing begins

Three testings of Israel, three temptations of Jesus

The testing continues—love the Lord your God with all your heart

DVD Discussion (6 minutes)

1. Using the map below, find the Judea Wilderness, which is the desert region in which the evil one most likely tempted Jesus.

How far is this desert from Jerusalem? Bethlehem? The Jordan River?

Deuteronomy— written [prophet] by Moses to new generation going into the promised land. last words

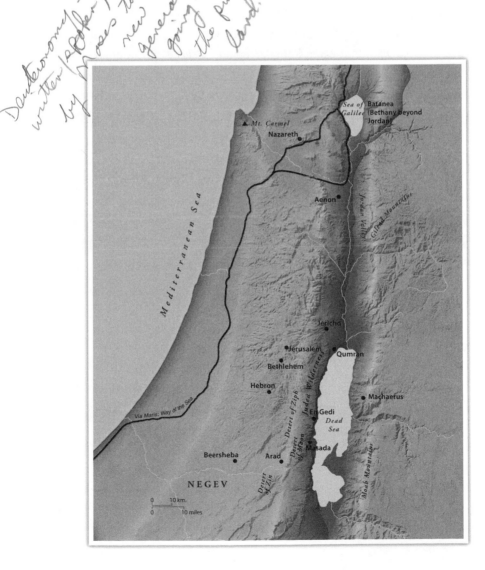

Into which other desert regions mentioned in the Bible does the Judea Wilderness lead?

DATA FILE
Desert Lands In and Near Ancient Israel

In the Hebrew Bible, desert is "God's land" in which he trained his people to live by every word that came from his mouth. Desert is also a metaphor of the difficult times in life during which God provides just enough to sustain us so that we learn to depend on him and trust him fully. Several desert regions in and near Israel played a key role in the lives of God's people during biblical times.

THE VAST DESERT REGIONS OF THE SINAI PENINSULA

The *Sinai Desert*, where the Israelites wandered for forty years, is the "vast and dreadful" desert of the exodus. It is the most severe desert region, and only God's miraculous provision enabled his people to survive there.

The *Negev Desert*, barely forty miles south of Jerusalem, has rolling desert pasture country in the north, rugged canyons in its central region, and extremely barren land in the south.

The *Judea Wilderness* lies between the populated areas of Israel and the Dead Sea. This desert is only a short walk away from the people—literally within sight—who live in Israel's central mountains. It is quite certain that Jesus was tempted in this desert.

2. As the video revealed how Jesus' testing in the desert paralleled that of the Israelites in the Sinai deserts during the exodus, what new understanding and appreciation did you gain for God's ongoing story of redemption?

   God doesn't give up — Jesus didn't fail. Both were tested + Jesus didn't fail

   What new understanding do you have concerning the importance of God's Word for his people of all times?

   The Word is a mighty weapon to battle satan — Put God first in everything.

3. For every temptation the evil one put before him, Jesus answered, "It is written ...." What did you learn from Jesus' knowledge of the Word of God and his example of commitment to live by <u>every word</u> that will help you to deal with the testing you face?

   Turn to the Word when you are tempted or unsure

4. The video teaching showed how the Hebrews, Jesus, and Jesus' disciples faced similar tests related to their commitment to walk in God's ways. In what ways do you think people today are tested regarding:

    a. Their commitment to live by every word that comes from the mouth of God?

    So many distractions – Very loud world.

    b. Their willingness to trust God with all aspects of their lives?

    Hard to trust anyone but yourself. finances

    c. Their faithfulness to "remember" God with all their heart, soul, and mind (strength, might)?

Small Group Bible Discovery and Discussion (15 minutes)

Baptized and Tested in the Desert

Although people are not inclined to go into the desert willingly, it is God's testing ground. It is where he gains the attention of his people so that they can hear his voice, participate in his training, and learn the lessons that will enable them to fulfill the mission he gives to them. That is why God took the Israelites into the desert and kept them there until they had learned to love him with all their heart, soul, and strength.

Before Jesus began his earthly ministry of proclaiming and demonstrating the kingdom of God to his world, he would have to go into the desert. He, too, would experience the lessons the Israelites learned there. The very words God gave to Israel in the desert became central in Jesus' confrontation with the devil, who intended to thwart God's plan to restore *shalom* to his broken creation.

1. What insight does 1 Corinthians 10:1 – 2 provide concerning the meaning of the crossing of the Red Sea to the Hebrew people?

    Submit to Moses — to Christ

    After the crossing of the Red Sea, how did the Hebrews respond? (See Exodus 15:1 – 7.) 18

    Praising the Lord

    In what sense do you think these former slaves had been reborn as God's chosen people and caught their first glimpse of the hope of the kingdom of heaven? (See Exodus 15:11 – 18.)

    Three days later, where were they and why? (See Exodus 15:22 – 27.)

2. After the Israelites' "Red Sea baptism," God tested them in the desert in order to prepare them for the great mission to which he had called them. How long did he test them? (See Deuteronomy 8:2.)

40 yrs

If God tested his chosen people for this long, how important do you think obedience and the advancement of his kingdom is to him?

How does this influence your perspective and attitude toward the time you have spent in the "desert" facing hardship?

THINK ABOUT IT
Why Does God Test His People?

The Jewish sages recognized God's sovereign reign over all things, but not all people acknowledge that reign. In order for the kingdom of God to advance and accomplish its work in the world, however, God's people must acknowledge his reign and enthrone him as their king by obeying his commands. Christian belief encompasses the same thought: those who commit to God acknowledge him as Lord and Savior and accept his reign by walking as Jesus walked (which was by obeying God's commands).

How do God's people learn to obey? Through testing! The Hebrew word translated "test" does not imply enticing to do wrong. It implies proving the quality of someone by experience — that is, to know experientially rather than simply by mental assent. God knew what was in Israel's heart, but he wanted to see them live out his reign in their lives, so he tested them to see if they would obey his instructions and depend on his word. These tests gave his people opportunities to strengthen their faith by putting it into practice.

Followers of Jesus in the West seldom view "testing" in this way. We listen to or read the Scriptures and then are invited to "believe" — to assent that we accept God's Word as true. Although God is certainly pleased with such belief, he also desires to see us practice our assent. Testing is his way of putting his people into situations where it becomes obvious whether or not their faith is genuine and shapes how they live.

Jesus' temptations (testing) pose difficult questions for people who believe that the Bible is the very Word of God. "How could Jesus as the Son of God be tempted?" "Can God sin?" (Obviously not.) "Could the sinless, fully human Jesus have sinned?" "Why did Jesus need to be tested?"

We know that Jesus was "tempted in every way, just as we are — yet was without sin" (Hebrews 4:15). This perspective does not deny his divine nature nor his sinless human nature. The foundational issue for Jesus — as was true for Adam and Eve and the ancient Israelites, and now for us — focused on acknowledging God as Lord and enthroning him by obedience to his Word. The temptations Jesus faced in his human nature were genuine. Like the temptation sinless Adam and Eve faced, Jesus' response to the desert temptations had the potential to undermine God's redemptive plan.

3. Jesus was the perfect candidate for John's baptism, which symbolized a person's purity and commitment to obedience. As Jesus came out of the water, what parted (or separated) and what was present? (See Matthew 3:13 – 17; Mark 1:9 – 11; Luke 3:21 – 22.)

In what way might this scene be an allusion to God bringing *shalom* out of chaos at creation? (See Genesis 1:1 – 2.)

Like Adam and Eve in the garden, Jesus had a God-given mission to fulfill. Like them, he began as God's sinless servant. What would someone who knew God's story expect to see happen after the symbolic "re-creation" at his baptism? (See Genesis 3:1 – 4; Mark 1:12 – 13.)

When the evil one tried to entice Jesus to abandon his commitment to walk in God's ways, how well did Jesus prove himself ready to fulfill his mission of proclaiming and demonstrating the kingdom of God? (See Matthew 4:1 – 11.)

FOR GREATER UNDERSTANDING
Patterns of Creation and Testing in God's Unfolding Story

When God created the universe, his Spirit brought order out of chaos by separating the waters of the formless deep (Genesis 1:1 – 9). In Hebrew, the word translated "Spirit" is *ruach,* which also means "breath" and "wind." After God completed his creation, the evil one tempted Adam and Eve to rebel against God's kingship.

Their sin destroyed the *shalom* of God's perfect created order, and chaos grew from generation to generation until God destroyed everything living on the earth in the great flood of Noah's day. For forty days, the floodwaters kept coming. After 150 additional days, the wind (God's *ruach*) began to cause the floodwaters to recede, which allowed life on earth to begin anew. After a time, however, Noah became drunk and fell into sin, and chaos was reintroduced (Genesis 9:20 – 27).

With great power, God freed the Hebrews from the chaos of slavery. When the "chaos" of the pursuing Egyptian army threatened to destroy them at the Red Sea, God used a "strong east wind" (*ruach*) to "divide" ("separate") the waters and give his people safe passage while destroying their enemies. The Hebrews, in a sense "baptized" by their passage through the sea, walked away as a new people. By enthroning God as their King and making a covenant to obey his commands, they embraced his mission of demonstrating the *shalom* of his kingdom to the world.

As the Israelites prepared to enter the Promised Land and live as the people God created them to be, they faced the chaos of the flooding Jordan River. Again, God "separated" water, and his people in a sense "passed through" a water baptism (Joshua 3:14 – 4:7) to enter the land as a "re-created" people who were committed to obeying all the ways of God.

As Jesus was coming out of the water after his baptism, heaven was "torn open" (separated, parted), and God's Spirit descended on him like a dove (Matthew 3:16; Mark 1:9 – 11). The Hebrew word used, *merachafet*, refers to the hovering motion of a dove that is reminiscent of the hovering Spirit of God at creation. After forty days of testing in the desert, Jesus began to teach about God's kingdom.

Faith Lesson (5 minutes)

At various times, God has begun a new creation on earth. Each time, he used his *ruach* to dispel chaos and bring a beautiful new reality into existence. But the world of chaos always seeks opportunities to destroy the *shalom* that God establishes. So desert times come:

- To test us and see if we do love the Lord our God with all our heart, soul, and mind (strength or might).
- To prepare us to live and proclaim the good news of the kingdom of heaven.

1. Those of us who are Christians today are often surprised
    when we find ourselves in the desert, especially when des-
    ert times come on the heels of spiritual triumph. Do you
    think Jesus, who knew and lived the Hebrew text, was sur-
    prised that the evil one tempted him immediately after his
    baptism? Why or why not?

    In what ways does Jesus' confident, unshakable attitude and
    example of faithful commitment to obeying God's Word
    show you how to handle such challenges in your life?

    With Jesus' example in mind, make a list of specific
    responses you can train yourself to follow when you face
    temptation and testing.

2. What has been your experience in dealing with personal
    "deserts" in your past?

    Did you recognize them for what they were at the time, and
    how do you view them differently today?

When you are in the "desert," to what extent are you able to confidently trust that God is who he says he is and can be depended upon to provide for you as you seek to obey him in every area of your life? And to what extent do you fail?

What have you learned about your walk with God through his testing and training in the "desert," and how have these experiences prepared you to be a stronger witness of his kingdom?

Closing (1 minute)

Read aloud together Matthew 22:36 – 40: " 'Teacher, which is the greatest commandment in the Law?' Jesus replied: "'Love the Lord your God with all your heart and with all your soul and with all your mind [strength].' This is the first and greatest commandment. And the second is like it: 'Love your neighbor as yourself.' All the Law and the Prophets hang on these two commandments.' "

Then pray together, thanking God for his Law — his words given in the desert — to teach and train his people to love him by living by his every word. Ask him to help you follow the example of Jesus who showed us how to live the *shema* and love God with all our heart, soul, and mind (strength).

Memorize

"Teacher, which is the greatest commandment in the Law?" Jesus replied: "'Love the Lord your God with all your heart and with all your soul and with all your mind [strength].' This is the first and greatest commandment. And the second is like it: 'Love your neighbor as yourself.' All the Law and the Prophets hang on these two commandments."

Matthew 22:36 – 40

Learning to Walk in the Way of the Lord

In-Depth Personal Study Sessions

Day One | Jesus' Relationship with the Desert

The Very Words of God

> *Jesus, full of the Holy Spirit, returned from the Jordan and was led by the Spirit in the desert, where for forty days he was tempted by the devil. He ate nothing during those days, and at the end of them he was hungry.*
>
> *Luke 4:1–2*

Bible Discovery

Jesus As Our Desert

God's plan to redeem the people who would be his instruments in bringing redemption to his world took shape in the deserts of the biblical world. The Torah, written originally for the Israelites who had been driven out of Egypt and into the deserts of Sinai, introduces the kingdom of heaven (God) — God's plan for redeeming his world. It describes in detail the origin of the religious system of God's people including priesthood, sacrificial system, tabernacle, ethical code, and institutions of prophet and king. Moses and Aaron, as paradigms for prophet and high priest respectively, have central roles in this desert story. One could say that the rest of the Hebrew Bible explains and develops God's purpose for his people as it is first introduced and based in the Torah.

So when Jesus — the Messiah, the Passover Lamb — came to accomplish his long-awaited work of redemption, there is a sense in which he *had* to spend time in the desert. Desert has always been a central theme in God's plan of redemption, and Jesus is presented as the one who fulfills in his person the rich desert experiences of God's ancient people.

During his earthly life, Jesus clearly became the fullness of nearly every significant concept, practice, and lesson prevalent among his people. In and through his redemptive work, we see an intimate relationship with his heavenly Father. In fact, everything in the experience of God's people, who have a necessary part in his redemptive plan, comes to fullness in Jesus. Jesus not only went into the desert, but in a real sense became the desert "experience" for us. His desert experience did for us the things the desert did for Israel.

1.   The Bible presents Jesus as the One who fulfills in his person the rich desert experiences of God's ancient people. In that sense, he is our "desert." Like the manna God "rained down from heaven" to feed his people in the desert, for example, Jesus is the bread of heaven who satisfies our hunger. Many such experiences that God gave the ancient Hebrews in the desert were completed in the person and work of Jesus. As you read the following portions of the text, (1) note the experiences, institutions, images, and themes that "connect" Jesus to the Hebrews' experience in the desert; (2) consider how the Hebrews' exodus experience formed the foundation for Jesus' redemptive work; and (3) note how Jesus fulfills and completes the Hebrews' desert experiences.

Text	How Jesus Fulfills the Desert Experiences of God's People
Ex. 16:4, 13–16, 31 John 6:32–35, 51–58	
Ex. 17:5–6; Jer. 2:13 John 4:7–14; 7:37–39	

continued on next page . . .

Text	How Jesus Fulfills the Desert Experiences of God's People
Num. 21:4–9 John 3:14–15	
Num. 12:3 Matt. 11:29	
Ex. 25:8–9 John 1:14[1]	
Ps. 77:20; 78:52; Num. 27:15–17 John 10:11, 14	
Deut. 18:17–20[2] John 1:21–25; 6:14; 7:40	
Lev. 16:6–10 Heb. 10:10–14; 13:12–13;	
Ex. 12:3–14, 21 John 1:29; Luke 22:14–16; John 13:1; 19:14–16	

FOR GREATER UNDERSTANDING

"Born" in the Desert to Advance the Kingdom of God

Truly God birthed his people in the desert. The patriarchs—Abraham, Isaac, and Jacob—lived at the edge of desert. Moses herded sheep in the desert for forty years before God called him to lead his people out of Egypt. David, God's role model for Israel's kings, lived in the desert herding sheep for years before becoming king. And the Israelites spent forty years in the desert being shaped by their God so that through their successes (and their failures) his purposes were fulfilled.

At the beginning of his ministry, Jesus the Messiah went into the desert. There, in a poignant portrayal of his love for his Father and his people, he willingly endured brutal desert heat and cold and lived without food for forty days. There the evil one, the tempter, sought to draw the Messiah away from the task of restoring God's *shalom* to all things through his death and resurrection.

Jesus' faithfulness during these temptations demonstrated his belief in the very nature of God—that God is worthy of complete trust and total commitment as the Torah declares (Deuteronomy 6:4 – 5). His steadfast commitment to pursue God's redemptive purpose for him—not his own purposes or those of the evil one—emphasized his commitment to accept God's mission without reservation. And after his temptations, Jesus emerged to proclaim that the kingdom of God (heaven) was at hand (Mark 1:12–15).

Followers of Jesus often focus on Israel's failures in the desert in order to explain the need for a greater Messiah. Even the Christian text reviews their disobedience during those forty years. But we must also remember that the Israelites, although imperfect, emerged from the desert having been shaped by their God for forty years. God continued to use them to prepare for the coming of Jesus, whose mission and ministry was the great climax to the history of God's people. And after Jesus fulfilled his messianic mission on earth, God continued to use flawed humans as his instruments in bringing the gospel message to a world in chaos.

continued on next page . . .

For two millennia, through success and glaring failure, God has used follow-ers of Jesus to bring untold numbers of people to his *shalom*. The climax of the mission that Jesus' followers today work hard to fulfill will be his second appearance to complete the work God has accomplished through all of his human partners since the days of Adam and Eve. Will we often fail? Yes. Will we be failures? No. By God's grace and our repentance he will forgive us and use even our failures to accomplish his purposes. By his power, we will often succeed in our mission. Like the Hebrews in the desert, we belong to the community God uses to advance the coming of his kingdom.

Reflection

In Exodus 4:22 – 23, God refers to his people, Israel, as his "firstborn son" whom he called out of Egypt and into the desert to worship him. (Remember, in the Hebrew Bible, "worship" encompasses obedience.) Yet his people did not love their heavenly Father "wholeheartedly" (Hosea 11:1 – 2). Their hearts were divided and uncommitted — ready to obey God to a point but no further.

Then God called Jesus, his one and only Son (John 3:16), out of Egypt and into the desert to worship him. Jesus was faithful where Israel, God's first son, had not been completely faithful. Jesus applied the lessons of Israel's testing in the desert, which were learned through failure, in order to resist temptation and obey. With all his heart, soul, and mind, he chose to live faithfully by every word from God's mouth. Thus Jesus fulfilled the work of redemp-tion that God originally introduced in the Torah.

Take time to review the experiences of Jesus and the Hebrews in the desert that you explored earlier in this study.

> In what ways do the exodus experiences help you to better understand the work of Jesus?
>
> How he lived out the kingdom of God?

What his redemptive work has done for you personally?

In what way(s) do these specific desert experiences help you to understand the ongoing work of redemption to which God has called all of his people, including you?

In what ways do they help you to recognize how to live out the life of the kingdom of God in your world?

In what ways do they help you to know how to choose obedience when you face temptation?

Day Two | Love the Lord with All Your Heart

The Very Words of God

> *But they continued to sin against him,*
> *   rebelling in the desert against the Most High.*
> *They willfully put God to the test*
> *   by demanding the food they craved.*
> *They spoke against God, saying,*
> *   "Can God spread a table in the desert?"*

> *Psalm 78:17–19*

Bible Discovery

Can God Be Trusted to Provide?

After they miraculously crossed the Red Sea and emerged, in a
sense, as a "new" people who acknowledged God as their king,
Moses led the Hebrews into the desert. They had seen God do
miraculous things on their behalf — the plagues in Egypt, the pillar
of cloud and fire, his destruction of Pharaoh's army. When they were
desperately thirsty, God turned the bitter water sweet at Marah
and then led them to springs and palm trees at Elim. Would that be
enough to satisfy them? Would they be content to trust in God's provision for them and live on his every word? Or did they have their
own ideas about what they wanted?

1. Why did the Israelites grumble against Aaron and Moses
    in the Desert of Sin? (See Exodus 16:1 - 5, 13 - 20; Psalm
    78:12 - 22, 29.)

    They left Egypt with dough for bread, flocks, and herds, so
    they weren't really starving. What appears to be the reason
    for their dissatisfaction?

    What was the "test" that God prepared related to their
    complaint?

    Was God's provision of the food they needed in any way
    dependent on their response to the test? Why or why not?

2. How did God want his people to respond to the test? (See Exodus 16:4 - 5.)

   What was he hoping the test would accomplish in their hearts? (See Deuteronomy 6:4 - 6; 8:2 - 3.)

   The Hebrew word *kol*, translated "all your heart" in Deuteronomy 6:5, means "totally," "absolutely everything," "completely." How does this help you to understand the kind of love God desires from his people?

3. Matthew recorded the temptations Jesus faced in the desert after his baptism. The first one mentioned occurred after Jesus' forty-day fast and, naturally, had to do with food.[3] What was the temptation (test), and how did Jesus respond? (See Matthew 4:1 - 4.)

   Which of the Israelites' experiences in the desert provides the context for Jesus' response? (See Exodus 16:2 - 5; Deuteronomy 8:3.)

What does Jesus' response reveal about his knowledge and understanding of the Hebrew Scriptures, and how strong a statement did he make about his commitment to live by the words of God?

Was it as important for Jesus to live by God's words and trust that God would provide for his needs as it was for the Israelites? Explain your answer.

PROFILE OF A SLANDERER

The Greek word translated "devil," like the Hebrew word translated "Satan," means "accuser" or "slanderer." Known as the "evil one" to the Jews, he is the eternal enemy of God. He is not just a force or power, but is a real spiritual being. Together with his evil followers, he works continually to undermine God's plan to restore *shalom*.

To clarify, the phrase "*If* you are the Son of God" implies "*Since* you are the Son of God." The evil one did not doubt Jesus' identity as the Son of God. Rather, he sought to tempt Jesus to use his supernatural power for his own benefit instead of trusting completely in God and his provision.

This first temptation concerned God and his purposes. It challenged his worthiness to receive all worship, obedience, and love. It brought into question God's trustworthiness and the wisdom of his redemptive plan. Would Jesus carry out God's plan in complete submission to his Father's will even if it meant great suffering? Or would he seek his own way to achieve that purpose?

Reflection

God gave the Bible to his people for our instruction. Take a few minutes to review the Hebrew (Old Testament) and Christian (New Testament) texts on living by God's every word. Note the similarities between the key words of Deuteronomy 8:2 – 5 and Matthew 4:1 – 4 (emphasis added):

> *Remember how the* Lord *your God* **led** *you all the way in the* **desert** *these* **forty** *years; to humble you and to* **test** *you in order to know what was in your heart, whether or not you would keep his commands. He humbled you, causing you to* **hunger** *and then feeding you with manna, which neither you nor your fathers had known, to teach you that* **man does not live on bread alone but on every word that comes from the mouth of the** Lord. *Your clothes did not wear out and your feet did not swell during these* **forty** *years. Know then in your heart that as a man disciplines his* **son**, *so the* Lord *your* **God** *disciplines you.*
>
> *Deuteronomy 8:2 – 5*

> *Then Jesus was* **led** *by the Spirit into the* **desert** *to be* **tempted** *by the devil. After fasting* **forty** *days and* **forty** *nights, he was* **hungry**. *The tempter came to him and said, "If you are the* **Son** *of* **God**, *tell these stones to become* **bread**." *Jesus answered, "It is written:* '**Man does not live on bread alone, but on every word that comes from the mouth of God.**'"
>
> *Matthew 4:1 – 4*

How does Matthew's use of these key words and phrases, patterned after Moses' account in Deuteronomy, connect the experiences of Israel and Jesus? (The Jewish people of Matthew's day, educated in the Torah, would likely have caught this allusion immediately.)[4]

In what way(s) do you think "testing," which in Hebrew can mean "tempt" as well as "prove," helps to develop the faith of God's people in him and in his Word — the Bible?

If you consider the whole account of God providing manna in the desert (Exodus 16:1 – 30), how did God's testing help to develop the faith of his people?

Do you think Jesus learned and grew in the practice of his faith as a result of the evil one's temptations? Why or why not?

In what ways has God taught and tested you regarding your commitment to totally and completely depend on him and live by his every word?

Memorize

He humbled you, causing you to hunger and then feeding you with manna, which neither you nor your fathers had known, to teach you that man does not live on bread alone but on every word that comes from the mouth of the LORD.

Deuteronomy 8:3

DID YOU KNOW?

In the ancient Near East, writers did not always record events in chronological order. Sometimes they ordered events according to themes or theological points. Matthew, for example, recorded the three temptations of Jesus in this order: "tell these stones to become bread," "throw yourself down," and "bow down and worship me." Luke switched the order of the last two temptations. Why?

Scholars suggest that Matthew's order is chronological and progresses from an "ordinary" test of trusting God for daily sustenance to God's protection and then to an "all-consuming" test of worshiping the devil. Jesus came up out of the water of the Jordan River and was sent into the desert. Then the evil one then took him to the highest point on the temple and finally to a "very high mountain." In this way, Matthew communicated the increasing level of rejection of God that the evil one proposed. Matthew's sequence also links the temptations directly to the ancient Hebrews' forty years in the desert, portrays Jesus as being completely faithful to the greatest command (versus Israel's unfaithfulness), and shows Jesus using God's words related to the Hebrews' lessons as his weapon against the evil one's attacks.

Luke, on the other hand, often focused on Jerusalem. His Gospel focuses on Jesus' journey to Jerusalem for the climax of his ministry. In Luke's second work, Acts, Jesus' followers spread out from Jerusalem into the whole world. It would be consistent, then, for Luke to record the temptations geographically — beginning in the desert, continuing on a high mountain, and ending with a test on the highest point of the temple in Jerusalem.

Day Three | Is the Lord Among Us or Not?

The Very Words of God

> *And he called the place Massah and Meribah because the Israelites quarreled and because they tested the LORD saying, "Is the LORD among us or not?"*

Exodus 17:7

Bible Discovery

Love the Lord by Entrusting Your Life (Soul) to Him

In Jesus' day, the Jewish understanding of "love the Lord with all your soul" meant that a person loved God and willingly entrusted his or her very life to him. It meant following him in complete obedience even if it required putting one's life at risk. When God led the Israelites to Rephidim, where there was no water, their willingness to entrust their lives to God was tested. Discover how Jesus used this experience to stand against the twisted way in which the evil one tried to tempt Jesus to sin by questioning his willingness to put his life in God's hands.

1. At Rephidim, where there was no water, how did the Israelites respond to their need? (See Exodus 17:1 – 7.)

    In what way did their "request" in this situation differ from the times they had expressed their needs previously? (See Exodus 14:10 – 12; 15:23 – 24; 16:2 – 3.)

If the Israelites weren't simply asking God to provide water, what bigger issue was at stake? (See Exodus 17:7.)

It appears that the Israelites tested God by demanding that he prove his presence and provide for them *before* they would trust him. In the Jewish context, they were refusing to entrust their lives — their souls — to God until he proved himself yet again. How did God respond to their demand? (See Deuteronomy 6:16.)

THINK ABOUT IT

In this temptation, Satan cleverly misquoted Psalm 91:11 that promised God's protection for those who walk in God's ways during the normal course of life (Psalm 91:1 – 2, 9 – 10; also Deuteronomy 8:6; 30:16). A suicidal act to demand that God prove his protection is not walking in his ways! One of Satan's common methods of temptation is to misquote God's words (Genesis 2:15 – 17; 3:1). The evil one's use of God's own words to tempt Jesus highlights the importance of our knowing the Bible well.

2. In Matthew's account, the evil one next took Jesus to the temple where God's presence lived and where God promised to protect his people. What did the evil one challenge Jesus to do to prove God's protection? (See Matthew 4:5 – 7.)

What words of the Bible did the evil one use in this temptation, and which ones did he leave out? (See Psalm 91:11 – 12.)

With which words of the Bible did Jesus refuse this temptation? (See Deuteronomy 6:16.)

How does Jesus' response show that he knew the true intent of the evil one's question? (Hint: To what desert test does Deuteronomy 6:16 refer?)

DATA FILE

Temptation on the "Wing" of the Temple

When the evil one tempted him, Jesus (God's only begotten Son) was in a sense reliving the story of Israel's (God's firstborn son) testing in the desert. Jesus faced the same tests to love God with all his heart, soul, and strength. He answered each of the evil one's tests by quoting from the lessons of the exodus.

For the second temptation by Matthew's accounting, Satan took Jesus to the temple, the most dramatic location that symbolized God's presence and promise to protect his people. There, on the highest point of the temple, he dared Jesus to jump and thereby demand that God prove his promises to be true. The Greek word translated "pinnacle" or "highest point" (Matthew 4:5) is *pterygion* (Hebrew: *kanaf*, meaning "wing" or "corner") and literally means "little wing."

This is the sole biblical reference to a temple "wing," and it is intriguing to consider why Satan took Jesus to the "wing" of the temple. Traditionally, the pinnacle of the temple is said to be the southeastern corner of the temple platform more than one hundred feet above the Kidron Valley. More recently, scholars have discovered the stone railing at the southwestern corner of the temple platform where the trumpet was blown and suggest that it is the pinnacle.

However, given the first-century Jews' intense focus on the Hebrew Scriptures, it seems more likely the location was connected to the temple sanctuary, the house of God itself. The Hebrew Bible compares God's protection of Israel during the exodus experience to that of an eagle that carried and protected its young with his wings (Exodus 19:4; Deuteronomy 32:9 – 11; Psalm 17:8; 61:4). In the sanctuary, God's presence lived between the *wings* of the cherubim on the ark of the covenant (Exodus 25:20), which was another symbol of God's protective care over his people. As he proposed his temptation, Satan quoted from Psalm 91, which in verses 2 – 4 describes God protection of his people with his wings. So when Satan dared Jesus to test God's protection, he took Jesus to the very symbol of God's promise to protect him. Certainly Matthew's Jewish readers recognized the connection between God's protective wings during the exodus and the temple "wing" where God's presence resided.

Reflection

First-century Jews knew the Hebrew Bible and that they must not test God by demanding that he demonstrate his protection *before* they would fully obey him. Jesus used the lesson of Israel's demand that God prove his protection in order to resist the same temptation. Jesus loved the Lord with all his soul. He did not demand that God prove his protection before obeying him. Instead, he willingly trusted God with his life — even a brutal death on a cross.

> When has it been tempting for you to demand that God prove himself before you are willing to step out in faith and trust him fully?

What kind of provision or protection have you wanted God to prove to you?

Which portions of the Scripture text already promise that God will meet your need and care for you in that area of your life? (If you don't know of any, look for them!)

Is God's Word enough "proof" for you that he will do what he has promised? Why or why not?

To what extent does knowing God's Word and obediently walking according to his commandments make you more willing to trust him?

Do you truly desire, with every fiber of your being, to love the Lord your God with all your soul?

Memorize

> *"Because he loves me," says the LORD, "I will rescue him;*
> *I will protect him, for he acknowledges my name.*
> *He will call upon me, and I will answer him;*
> *I will be with him in trouble,*
> *I will deliver him and honor him."*

> *Psalm 91:14 – 15*

Day Four | Will You Love God with All Your Strength?

The Very Words of God

> *When the LORD your God brings you into the land he swore to your*
> *fathers, to Abraham, Isaac and Jacob, to give you — a land with large,*
> *flourishing cities you did not build, houses filled with all kinds of good*
> *things you did not provide, wells you did not dig, and vineyards and*
> *olive groves you did not plant — then when you eat and are satisfied, be*
> *careful that you do not forget the LORD, who brought you out of Egypt,*
> *out of the land of slavery.*

> *Deuteronomy 6:10 – 12*

Bible Discovery

The Test of Total Commitment

To love God with all our strength means to trust him and not our own efforts (important though they may be) for everything we need. Everything we do is to be motivated by wholehearted, loving devotion to God rather than a striving to meet our needs for ourselves. To love God with all our strength is to remember every day that we are dependent on him and to testify that everything we have is a gift from him. The moment we begin to live in our own strength and take credit for what we have, we "forget" him. We stop loving God with all our strength and deny his sovereignty — the first step toward idolatry.

1. When Moses gave his final speech before he died, what "test" did he say the Israelites would face in Canaan? (See Deuteronomy 6:10 – 12; 8:10 – 20.)

    What would the Israelites be tempted to do if they "forgot" the Lord, and what would be the consequences? (See Deuteronomy 6:13 – 15; 8:17 – 19.)

    Remember, in a Jewish way of thinking, the kingdom of God comes when his people acknowledge him as Lord and enthrone him as their King by living in obedience to his every word. With that in mind, read Deuteronomy 6:13. What was God asking his people to do by "remembering" him (v. 12), and why was it so important?

2. For the third temptation, which tested Jesus' total commitment to God, where did the evil one take him? (See Matthew 4:8 – 9.)

3. Although the mountain of Jesus' temptation isn't named, there are striking parallels to Moses' story on Mount Nebo, which God commanded Moses to climb on the last day of his life. What happened on Mount Nebo gives valuable insight into the nature of the evil one's temptation.

    a.   What did God show Moses from the top of that mountain? (See Deuteronomy 34:1 – 3.)

    b.   What did God say he would do with that land? (See Deuteronomy 34:4.)

    c.   What did Satan show Jesus from the top of the mountain? (See Matthew 4:8.)

    d.   What did Satan say he would do if Jesus worshiped him? (See Matthew 4:9.)

3.   Who has sole authority over creation, including the ability to give land and kingdoms? (See Jeremiah 27:5; Daniel 7:13 – 14.)

In what ways was the evil one challenging God's sovereignty — his right to be worshiped and worshiped exclusively — when he offered the kingdoms of earth to Jesus?

4. Considering that Jesus could have completely destroyed Satan for his blasphemy, what is striking about how he responded to the evil one? (See Matthew 4:10.)

How does Jesus' "it is written" response connect this temptation to the future "test" about which Moses warned the Israelites in Deuteronomy 6:13?

How does Jesus' response to Satan's proposal to worship him instead of God help you to better understand what was at stake for Israel if they "forgot" God?

DID YOU KNOW?

God redeems his people by grace, and he desires that they respond to him by calling him Lord and extending his reign through obedience to his commands. For a faithful Jew, reciting the *shema* (Deuteronomy 6:4–9) is the way one accepts God's kingship and expresses devotion to keeping his commandments. It is the public witness, to God and to one's community, of accepting the obligations of the covenant God made with his people. Saying *shema* is a daily commitment to love God by keeping his commandments. It is impossible to exaggerate the importance of this daily profession that continues from ancient times to the present. The *shema* is the first passage of Scripture a Jewish child is taught, the first and last Scripture recited every day, and the Scripture one hopes to recite on one's deathbed just before meeting God. Truly it was — and still is — the greatest commandment.

Reflection

Jesus loved the Lord with all his might! For first-century Jews, the *shema* (Deuteronomy 6:4 – 9) was the heart of God's revelation — the greatest commandment — for his people. They understood that their ancestors had not been completely faithful to that powerful command. Israel had not learned to love God with *all* of their being. But they believed that when Messiah came, he would show everyone — Israel and the nations of the world — how to live by that creed. And they were right!

The *shema* influenced everything Jesus said and did. When he was asked to identify the greatest commandment, he identified the *shema* (Matthew 22:35 – 38). And so it is for God's people today. To live the *shema* is to enthrone God as King. It is the key to living a life that demonstrates the kingdom of God.

Review in your mind Israel's testings and Jesus' temptations. Take note of what is required to love the Lord with all your heart, all your soul, and all your mind (strength).

What heart, soul, and strength issues are being tested in your life?

Which written words of God do you need to remember and obey in order to strengthen your faith and stand against temptation in each of these areas?

Jesus, unlike the Israelites, lived out the *shema* by using God's written Word against the powers of evil.

In what ways has Jesus' example encouraged you to learn God's words and live by them every day?

Do you know the Bible well enough to use it to walk on God's "path" and resist evil?

Memorize

Hear, O Israel: The LORD our God, the LORD is one. Love the LORD your God with all your heart and with all your soul and with all your strength.

Deuteronomy 6:4–5

DATA FILE
Forty Days of Fasting

In total devotion to their walk with God and the mission God had given to them, Moses, Elijah, and Jesus share a common experience no other biblical characters have faced: forty days of fasting in the desert. On two occasions, Moses fasted for forty days on Mount Sinai and evidently survived only through God's intervention. Although Scripture does not specifically use the word "fasted," Elijah put himself completely into God's care and walked for forty days and nights in the desert — apparently not even knowing where he was to go. His only sustenance was food the angel gave him before he started his journey.

Moses and Elijah fasted in complete dependence on, and submission to, God, who miraculously sustained them. Jesus followed their pattern—remaining completely devoted and submissive to his heavenly Father and the mission to which he had been called. His complete dependence on and trust in God during forty days in the desert is an example of obedience learned through suffering. It provides a challenge and encouragement for disciples of Jesus today who commit to walking as Jesus did (1 John 2:6).

Day Five | The Temptations Kept Coming

The Very Words of God

> *When the devil had finished all this tempting, he left him until an opportune time.*
>
> **Luke 4:13**

Bible Discovery

The Evil One Does Not Give Up

After the third temptation in the desert, the evil one left Jesus. One might think that the devil was so thoroughly defeated during this forty-day period that he would leave Jesus alone. After all, Jesus — physically weakened after those arduous days in the desert with no food — had been strong enough to use the Torah brilliantly and remain completely devoted to God! But Satan did not leave Jesus alone, nor has he stopped tempting followers of Jesus.

1. With what significant phrase regarding the evil one did Luke conclude his account of Jesus' temptations? (See Luke 4:13.)

Why do you think Satan remained determined to tempt Jesus?

Which events in Jesus' life indicate that Satan remained intent on stopping the advancement of the kingdom of God?

2.   Those "opportune" times for Satan to tempt Jesus certainly came. Even though the evil one's presence and the word "temptation" are not mentioned, specific situations raised the same issues related to loving God that had been raised when Jesus (as well as the Israelites) was tempted in the desert.

Text	The Situation	The "Temptation" He Could Have Chosen
Mark 3:20–21, 31–35; John 7:1–5		To not love God with all his heart
Luke 13:31–33		To not love God with all his soul (life)
John 6:1–15		To not love God with all his strength (mind)

3.   Jesus is the ultimate example of complete devotion to God and, as such, provides the pattern for those of us who follow him to face our temptations.

   a.   How can we benefit from the temptations Jesus faced? (See Hebrews 2:14 – 18; 4:14 – 16.)

    b.   What warnings and encouragement does God's Word provide to help prepare us for the temptations we will face? (See 1 Corinthians 10:13; Ephesians 6:16; James 4:7; 1 Peter 5:8 – 10; 1 John 5:18 – 20.)

    c.   What did God provide to strengthen Jesus before his temptations, and what will he provide for followers of Jesus today? (See Matthew 4:1; Ephesians 3:16 – 17.)

Reflection

The Bible reveals that the evil one will tempt those who follow Jesus. Even though Satan was soundly rejected by Jesus and his use of the Torah — the very words of God — he will never stop trying to defeat God's plans. He is still determined to prevent God's people from loving God with *all* their hearts, *all* their soul, and *all* their strength and mind. If you strive to walk as Jesus walked (1 John 2:6), you will be tested ... repeatedly.

Which is the hardest area of temptation for you? Being totally, wholeheartedly devoted to God with no divided loyalties? Being willing to trust God completely regardless of personal risk? Or, being willing to completely trust in God's provision and take no credit for your own abilities, possessions, or successes?

As you consider Jesus' example and the help he provides for handling temptation, what do you find is most helpful in preparing and strengthening yourself to face temptation?

In what ways might you handle temptations differently as a result of what you have learned through this study?

Memorize

This, then, is how you should pray: "Our Father in heaven, hallowed be your name, your kingdom come, your will be done on earth as it is in heaven. Give us today our daily bread. Forgive us our debts, as we also have forgiven our debtors. And lead us not into temptation, but deliver us from the evil one."

Matthew 6:9 – 13

THE LAST PASSOVER

The ministry of Jesus the Messiah is fundamentally linked to the exodus experiences of the Jewish people. At Mount Sinai Israel received the Torah, the intimate covenant between God and his people (his bride) that Jesus came to fulfill. Jesus was the bridegroom who gave his life for his bride. He was both priest and sacrifice, the symbolic scapegoat that had been burdened with the people's sins and taken outside the community to die. God brought Israel out of Egyptian bondage to become a kingdom of priests (Exodus 19:6), and Jesus' sacrifice brought people out of spiritual bondage to become a royal priesthood (1 Peter 2:9).

Little in Jesus' mission is not somehow rooted in, predicted by, or pictured in God's deliverance of Israel from Egypt. Many events of the exodus and Moses' life are echoed in the life of Jesus — the prophet like Moses whom God promised would come. Jesus escaped the threat of a pagan king, became the Shepherd of God's flock, led the Twelve, supplied bread from heaven, "tabernacled" among his people, was lifted up like a snake on a pole, went to a mountain to receive revelation from God, spent forty days fasting in the desert, provided "living water," and offered his life in the place of sinners.

But no exodus experience or revelation is more central to Jesus' mission than the Passover — Israel's deliverance and the meal by which the Jewish people have relived their deliverance ever since. According to the Gospel writers, Jesus celebrated his last Passover seder ("Last Supper") meal with his disciples. Then, as the Passover Lamb, he was killed so that his blood would deliver humankind from the bondage of sin.

When viewed in light of the exodus story, Jesus' actions and teachings during his celebration of the seder become increasingly dramatic and poignant. Passover and its rituals highlight the significance of Judas' betrayal, washing the disciples' feet, and the disciples' questions. The more we know about the experiences and practices of the Israelites as they relived the exodus through Passover, the more profound and moving Jesus' last hours before his crucifixion become.

This should not surprise us. God has only one story — to restore the *shalom* he originally created to all things, especially to the human race. Passover is a foundational element in this story of God's redemption. The Lord commanded Israel to commemorate the terrible and wonderful events of their deliverance from Egypt from generation to generation by celebrating Passover.

The Last Supper — celebrated on Passover and as a Passover — and Jesus' crucifixion and resurrection three days later are the culminating acts of the ministry of Jesus the Messiah. Although it is seldom commemorated in the context of Passover, the "Lord's Supper" finds its richest and most profound meaning when viewed as the completion of the redemptive process God began when he delivered the Hebrews from Egypt. No wonder Jesus instructed his disciples to celebrate it as he did in remembrance of him.

Opening Thoughts (3 minutes)

The Very Words of God

> *Christ, our Passover lamb, has been sacrificed. Therefore let us keep the Festival, not with the old yeast, the yeast of malice and wickedness, but with bread without yeast, the bread of sincerity and truth.*

> *1 Corinthians 5:7*

Think About It

People hold celebrations and festivals for a variety of reasons — to commemorate an historical event, to honor an influential person, to observe a religious ritual, or to celebrate a good harvest. Even a stranger who knows nothing about the reason for a particular event may enjoy the festivities. But how much more meaningful is it if the person knows the background of the celebration, or better yet, is an active participant or has a personal connection to what is being celebrated?

How "connected" would you say you are to the full significance of the "Last Supper," that is rooted in the Passover seder as it has been celebrated by Jewish people for millennia? *We teach the real significance of Jesus's body + blood*

DVD Notes (32 minutes)

Passover—a celebration to "remember"

The "Last Supper"—was it a Passover seder?

Who sat where?

The four promises (cups) of Passover:

    I will bring you out

    I will set you free

    I will redeem you

    I will take you

Dipping into the bitter herbs

DVD Discussion (6 minutes)

1. Since the first Passover in Egypt, God's chosen people have faithfully celebrated it wherever they have lived — in the deserts of Sinai during the exodus, in Jerusalem where God's presence resided in the temple, and in their homes in communities scattered around the world. During Jesus' time, pilgrims gathered in Jerusalem in huge numbers to sacrifice their Passover lambs and to celebrate the meal commemorating their ancestors' deliverance from Egypt. Jesus, of course, went to Jerusalem to celebrate his last Passover and complete his mission on earth by being the sacrificial Passover Lamb for all humanity.

    Using the map of Jerusalem on page 176, locate Jesus' activities during that Passover week (and after). Later, on your own, you will want to read the Bible passages that tell the story.

    • **Sunday:** Jesus' triumphal entry from *Bethany* (a village east of the Mount of Olives) on the road to the *Mount of Olives*, across the *Kidron Valley*, and up to the *temple mount* (Matthew 21:1 – 11); Jesus expelled merchants from the *temple* and returned to *Bethany* (Matthew 21.12 – 17).

    • **Monday through Wednesday:** Jesus taught in the *temple courts* (Matthew 21:23 – 45); was anointed at *Bethany* (Matthew 26:6 – 13); stayed overnight on the *Mount of Olives*, probably at *Gethsemane* (Luke 21:37), before returning to the temple.

    • **Thursday**: Jesus celebrated Passover, probably in the *Upper City* (Matthew 26:17 – 35); prayed at *Gethsemane* and was arrested (Matthew 26:36 – 56); was interrogated by Sanhedrin and betrayed by Peter, likely in the *Upper City* (Matthew 26:57 – 75); was tried by Herod and Pilate, probably at *Herod's palace* in the *Upper City* (Matthew 27:11 – 31; Luke 23:1 – 23).

    • **Friday**: Jesus is crucified and buried, likely in the *New City* at traditional *Golgotha* (Matthew 27:32 – 61).

    • **Sunday:** Jesus rose from the dead, likely near traditional *Golgotha* (Matthew 28:1 – 10).

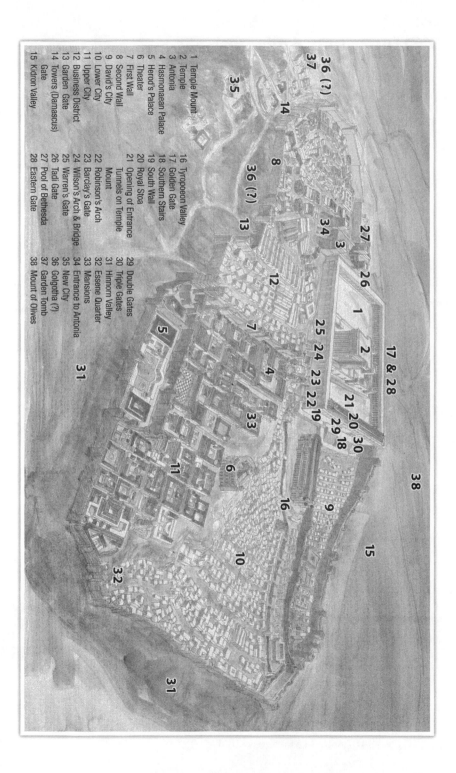

1 Temple Mount
2 Temple
3 Antonia
4 Hasmonaean Palace
5 Herod's Palace
6 Theater
7 First Wall
8 Second Wall
9 David's City
10 Lower City
11 Upper City
12 Business District
13 Garden Gate
14 Towers (Damascus) Gate
15 Kidron Valley

16 Tyropoeon Valley
17 Golden Gate
18 Southern Gate
19 South Wall
20 Royal Stoa
21 Opening of Entrance Tunnels on Temple Mount
22 Robinson's Arch
23 Barclay's Gate
24 Wilson's Arch & Bridge
25 Warren's Gate
26 Tadi Gate
27 Pool of Bethesda
28 Eastern Gate

29 Double Gates
30 Triple Gates
31 Hinnom Valley
32 Essene Quarter
33 Mansions
34 Entrance to Antonia
35 New City
36 Golgotha (?)
37 Garden Tomb
38 Mount of Olives

- **Forty days after Passover:** Jesus ascended from the *Mount of Olives* (Acts 1:1 – 11); disciples met together daily in *temple courts* (Acts 2:42 – 46).

- **Fifty days after Passover—Pentecost:** God's Spirit left the *temple* and rested on the community of Jesus' followers, probably on the *temple mount* (Acts 2:1 – 12).

2. In order to comprehend the redemptive work God accomplished for the Hebrews and later for all humanity through Jesus, it is helpful to understand the cultural meaning and connections between the first Passover and Jesus' meal with his disciples the night before his crucifixion. Think about what you learned through the video and discuss how it has broadened your understanding of the Passover seder and deepened the significance of the Lord's Supper for you. Consider:

    The meal as a reminder of reconciliation between God and people and between people and people

    a. The biblical meaning of "remember"

    b. The connection between God's promises and the cups of wine

    c. Jesus using unleavened bread as a representation of his body

    d. Jesus as the Passover Lamb

JESUS SET HIS FACE TOWARD JERUSALEM

Jesus conducted much of his teaching ministry in Galilee among devout Jews who were deeply committed to living by God's words in the Hebrew Bible. Large crowds gathered to hear him interpret God's words as he proclaimed that the kingdom of heaven (God) was among them. But when he visited Jerusalem to keep the festivals as God had commanded, his confrontations with certain religious rulers made him unpopular with the corrupt Sadducees who dominated Jerusalem and the temple by decree of King Herod and Rome. For this reason, Jesus and his disciples were always in danger in Jerusalem.

Despite the risk, Jesus still traveled from Galilee to Jerusalem to attend his last Passover. He refused to be deterred either by those he met along the way or by his disciples (Matthew 16:21–28). Knowing the danger and that this would be his last visit to Jerusalem, Jesus challenged his disciples to go with him. They would face great risks, but their reward would be even greater. They agreed and arrived in Jerusalem as Passover was about to begin, providing a context for Jesus' redemptive work that his Father had been preparing for more than a millennium. The Passover Lamb had come to Passover!

Small Group Bible Discovery and Discussion (14 minutes)

The Last Supper as a Fellowship Meal

The connections between Jesus' redemptive death and the first Passover in Egypt are intricate and powerful, and none is more significant than the last Passover seder[1] that Jesus celebrated with his disciples in the upper room. Before trying to grasp the deep meaning of the Last Supper, we must explore the significance of a "shared" or "fellowship" meal within the culture and religious practices of the people of the Bible.[2] Fellowship meals were a way to express the *shalom* (unity and harmony) of a restored covenantal relationship between people and between God and his people.

In the beginning, God created people to be in a covenantal relationship with him. Adam and Eve's sin broke that relationship, but throughout history God has been working to restore it. Thus God entered into a covenant with Abraham and his descendants, and through them with all people. Consistent with Middle Eastern customs, God shared fellowship meals with his people as a celebration of and commitment to their restored relationship. The covenantal meals described in the Bible provide the context for the Passover, which Jesus used to create the covenantal meal his followers celebrate to "remember" him.[3]

1. When Abraham's son, Isaac, lived in the land of the Philistines, he became so wealthy and powerful that the Philistines envied him (Genesis 26). They filled Isaac's wells repeatedly, forcing him to move away. Eventually Abimelech, king of the Philistines, had a change of heart and wanted to reconcile. How did Isaac and Abimelech celebrate their reconciliation, and what did it mean to them? (See Genesis 26:26 – 31.) *a covenant meal*

DID YOU KNOW?

For thousands of years, individuals, families, and tribes in Eastern cultures (Africa, Asia, the Middle East) have used a shared meal as a way to reconcile conflicts and as a sign of resolved conflict, forgiveness, mutual respect and acceptance, and friendship. That custom still continues.[4] In Eastern cultures, harmony between people is not simply a matter of laws but a relationship of the heart. In order to create or reestablish harmonious relationships, involved parties eat a meal together to celebrate their reconciliation and to covenant not to seek revenge in the future. After the meal, neither party will ever bring up past offenses.

2. After God delivered his people from slavery in Egypt, he expressed his love for them by establishing a covenantal relationship at Mount Sinai that is described as a marriage (Jeremiah 2:2; Hosea 2:14–20). The relationship between God and his people was "consummated" by burnt offerings, fellowship offerings, and the people's agreement to obey the book of the covenant. What amazing thing did God then do with the elders of Israel to confirm the relationship that existed between them? (See Exodus 24:1–11.)

Covenant made new.

Imagine being invited to a banquet in the presence of God! What impact do you think this "fellowship" meal had on the ancient Israelites and why? *Awe, veneration – feast w/God – your sins are forgiven – shed for you*

3. The regulations God established for fellowship offerings are recorded in Leviticus 3 and 7:11–38.

   a. What was the reason for a fellowship offering, and who shared in God's *shalom* through this celebration? (See Leviticus 7:11–15.)

   b. What do you think it meant for God's ancient people to be able to participate in a fellowship meal — a celebration of reconciliation, acceptance, and friendship — with a priest and their God?

THINK ABOUT IT
The Fellowship Offerings

At Sinai, God established the sacrificial system that removed the guilt of Israel's sin and formed the basis of God's forgiveness. Of the major sacrifices (guilt, burnt, sin, grain, and fellowship), the fellowship offering is the only one in which the worshiper eats a part of the sacrifice. Everyone shares God's *shalom* during this meal—the Lord, the priest, and the worshiper.

The fellowship offering reenacted the ceremony of Israel's elders eating and drinking in God's presence on Mount Sinai, which expressed their relationship with the powerful God who brought them out of Egypt. Every time a Jewish family brought an animal for a fellowship offering at the temple, they and the sacrificing priest would share a fellowship meal by eating the meat but burning the best portions as an offering to the Lord. This was viewed as a communal meal with God—just as if he were present at the table with them as he was on Mount Sinai!

4. Fellowship meals, a part of Jewish festivals commemorating God's faithfulness and love toward his people, were also celebrated when God's people faithfully completed a God-given task.

   a. What did the Israelites celebrate on the plains of Jericho after they crossed the Jordan River? (See Joshua 4:19 – 5:12, especially 5:10.) How many examples of reconciliation, faithfulness, and harmony in the covenant relationship between God and his people do you notice in this passage? Imagine what a celebration it must have been!

b. Based on what took place after Solomon's dedication of
God's temple in Jerusalem, how would you describe the
shalom of the covenant relationship between God and
his people? (Remember, a fellowship meal accompanies
fellowship offerings.) (See 1 Kings 8:62–66.) For how
many days did the people celebrate, and do you think
they believed that God was present with them as he had
been at Mount Sinai? Why or why not?

DID YOU KNOW?
There Is a Fellowship Meal to Come

One glorious day, as Isaiah 25:6–9 describes, *shalom* will come. God's
fellowship with people from all nations—Jew as well as Gentile—will be fully
restored. He will remove the burial shroud of death that covers his people and
will wipe away every tear. God will dwell with his people and they will sit down
with one another. At a banquet with fine food and wine, they will celebrate the
wedding feast of the Lamb forever!

Faith Lesson (4 minutes)

The first Passover did not involve a sacrifice to restore the relationship between God and his people; it involved the sacrifice of a
year-old lamb so that its blood painted on the doorframe of a house
would deliver the firstborn inside from the death angel. Future Passover celebrations, however, involved the sacrifice of Passover lambs
to the Lord (Deuteronomy 16:1–4) followed by a covenant meal
in Jerusalem, where God placed his name. So the Passover seder
became a fellowship meal that celebrated the covenant relationship
between the Lord and his people made possible through the sacrificial lamb.

Since Jesus came as the Lamb of God who would die in order to deliver humankind from bondage to sin, it is not surprising that he chose the Passover seder as the model for the covenant meal by which future generations would remember his redemptive work. In the upper room, Jesus focused the fellowship meal of Passover on his redemptive work as Messiah. What a profound way to commemorate this reconciliation!

1. Through Jesus' sacrifice, those of us who receive him as Lord and Savior enter into a new covenant relationship with God — forgiven of our sins and fully reconciled. We become part of his family, part of the community of faith. When we eat the Lord's Supper, we participate in a fellowship meal that confirms and portrays our reconciled relationship with God.

    a. When you have celebrated the Lord's Supper (Communion; Holy Eucharist), how aware have you been of your reconciliation with God that was made possible through Jesus' redeeming work?

    b. How has what you have learned about the fellowship meal and Passover seder deepened the meaning of your covenant relationship with God and the significance of the Lord's Supper in your daily life?

    c. When you celebrate the Lord's Supper, to what extent do you experience the excitement and joy of celebrating a fellowship meal with God as the Israelites did at Mount

Sinai, at the crossing of the Jordan River, and at the dedication of God's temple?

2. If we follow Jesus and have been reconciled to God as part of his community of people, what must we remember regarding our relationship with one another as we participate in the Lord's Supper — a fellowship meal? (See Romans 12:5; 1 Corinthians 12:12 – 13, 25 – 26.)

In what ways does your celebration of the Lord's Supper express the *shalom* (unity and harmony) of a restored covenantal relationship between people and between God and his people?

Do you think Jesus the Messiah would want any division or bitterness to exist among people who celebrate the reconciliation for which he gave his life? Why or why not?

In what relationship(s) in the community of God's people do you need to seek reconciliation and unity?

Closing (1 minute)

Read together Colossians 3:12 – 14: "Therefore, as God's chosen people, holy and dearly loved, clothe yourselves with compassion, kindness, humility, gentleness and patience. Bear with each other and forgive whatever grievances you may have against one another. Forgive as the Lord forgave you. And over all these virtues put on love, which binds them all together in perfect unity."

Then pray, thanking God for his sacrifice, longsuffering, and faithfulness in providing a way of redemption and reconciliation for the human race. Express to him your desire to follow his example of forgiveness and love for the unity of his people.

Memorize

Therefore, as God's chosen people, holy and dearly loved, clothe yourselves with compassion, kindness, humility, gentleness and patience. Bear with each other and forgive whatever grievances you may have against one another. Forgive as the Lord forgave you. And over all these virtues put on love, which binds them all together in perfect unity.

Colossians 3:12 – 14

Learning to Walk in the Way of the Lord

In-Depth Personal Study Sessions

Day One | Learning to "Remember"

The Very Words of God

> *The Lord Jesus, on the night he was betrayed, took bread, and when he had given thanks, he broke it and said, "This is my body, which is for you; do this in remembrance of me." In the same way, after supper he took the cup, saying, "This cup is the new covenant in my blood; do this, whenever you drink it, in remembrance of me."*
>
> 1 Corinthians 11:23–25

Bible Discovery

What Does it Mean to "Remember"?

The Bible is filled with exhortations to "remember." God remembers, Israel must remember, and during his last Passover Jesus instructed his disciples to do as he did in order to remember. To people in the West, remembering is merely intellectual recall (i.e., "Remember the meeting tonight"). To the ancient people of the Bible, remembering was to recall *and* to relive a past experience as if you were there *and* to act accordingly in obedience. To remember in a biblical sense involves intense focus on something or someone in the past that leads to an active response today.

When God commanded the Israelites to remember (in Hebrew, *zakar*, meaning "commemorate") the Passover (Exodus 12:14), he was not simply telling them to recall it. He wanted them to relive it as if they were there so that his amazing acts of deliverance would continue to shape them. And for thousands of years, that Passover night has remained real. Generations of Jews have learned to say, "I do this [celebrate Passover] because of what the LORD did for me when I came out of Egypt" (Exodus 13:8). By remembering in this way what God has done in the past, the significance and effects of God's faithfulness are brought continually into the present.

1. The infinite Creator God is completely unaffected by time and space, so when the Bible states that he "remembered" or "forgot" something, it does not mean that God's mind has limitations. It means that as God thinks about his people and his covenant with them, he is faithful to act and to fulfill his promises.

    a. In each of the following examples, what did God remember, and what action(s) resulted?

Text	What God Remembered—and the Action(s) He Took as a Result
Gen. 8:1; 9:8–16	
Num. 10:1–9	
Deut. 9:25–27; Gen. 17:3–8, 19–21	
Ps. 105:7–45	
Jer. 31:31–34 (Heb. 8:10–12)	
Hos. 9:1, 9	
Luke 1:46–55	

    b. Sometimes God chooses not to remember — to not act on things in his memory. What are some things God did not remember?

Text	What God Chose Not to Remember— and the Action(s) He Took as a Result
Isa. 43:25	
Jer. 31:31–34 (Heb. 8:10–12)	
Ezek. 33:13–16	

   c.   What encouragement do you find in what God remembers and what he chooses not to remember? Why?

2.   Many commands in the Bible instruct God's people to remember. For each of the following passages, write down what God's people were to remember, and the action that God would expect in response to each.

Numbers 15:37 – 41

Deuteronomy 4:10 – 14; 5:15; 7:17 – 21

Joshua 1:13 – 15

Psalm 105:5 – 6

Malachi 4:4

3. *Remembering* was not to be a morbid "dwelling on the past." Rather, the festivals God commanded played a central function in worship. They helped God's people to recall and identify with their history, to relive the experience of God's faithfulness, and to move forward in faithful response because they had participated in that history. The times, activities, and even locations of worship often enhanced Israel's recall and enabled God's people to relive and internalize his redemptive work. Of the annual festivals that God wanted his people to remember (Leviticus 23), Passover and the Feast of Unleavened Bread were the most focused on "remembering." Read Exodus 12:1 – 20; 13:1 – 10; Leviticus 23:4 – 8; and Deuteronomy 16:1 – 8 and consider the specific practices of these festivals that would help them to remember, relive, and respond as God desired.

    a. The specific time of year, day, and time of day Passover was to begin

    b. How they were to eat the Passover meal, what they were to eat, and for how long

    c. The consecration of the firstborn and the importance of the observance

    d.   Why they were to eat unleavened bread, what unleavened bread symbolized, where they were to celebrate

    e.   How would your obedience to these commands keep what God had done for you fresh in your mind and alive in your heart, and how would observing the festival move you toward obeying all of God's commands?

Reflection

Like Moses before him, Jesus said to his followers (at the Last Supper), "Do this to remember me" (1 Corinthians 11:24 MSG). His command to imitate his actions in order to remember him called his disciples to relive that moment and act accordingly. More than a millennium of history had prepared them to understand what that involved. *Remembering* should be as important to those of us who follow Jesus today as it was to the ancient Israelites and to Jesus' disciples.

God wants us to celebrate the Lord's Supper so that we'll remember — *zakar* — who we are and will live as his redeemed people. We were in bondage to sin until God's redeeming love delivered us, setting us free to worship and obey him. To remember is to live in passionate obedience to him because his grace is significant in our lives. If we are tempted to worship other gods, including money or status, we remember that the blood of the Lamb set us free. If we find ourselves disrespecting other people or using them selfishly rather than serving them, we remember that the blood of the Lamb has set us free. If we realize that we are living to please ourselves rather than to glorify God, we remember that the blood of the Lamb set us free. With each remembrance, we rededicate ourselves to live out our identity as redeemed people of God. Remember!

To what extent is remembering what God has done essential to your knowing him intimately and responding to him in whole-hearted obedience?

In what way(s) is the Eastern way of remembering — *zakar* — God, his work in the world, and the successes and failures of his people throughout history essential to true spiritual growth?

When we, as the community of God's people, remember what God has done and respond with appropriate action, in what ways is our personal walk with him strengthened? In what ways do our faith communities shine brighter in a spiritually dark world?

How might we, as followers of Jesus today, benefit from celebrating God's festivals of remembrance even though God no longer commands us to do so?

How will remembering Jesus' sacrifice as the Passover Lamb shape your day today? Shape your days from this time forward?

Memorize

I will remember the deeds of the LORD;
> *yes, I will remember your miracles of long ago.*
I will meditate on all your works
> *and consider all your mighty deeds.*

Psalm 77:11 – 12

FOR FUTURE STUDY

Jesus commanded his followers to "remember" his words and actions. The Lord's Supper became a central practice in enabling them to remember, just as Passover had done and continues to do for the Jewish people. To ponder what remembering him involves, read Matthew 7:21 – 27; Luke 24:6, 8; John 2:20 – 22; 12:16; 14:23, 26; 16:1 – 4; Romans 15:14 – 16; 2 Timothy 2:8; and 2 Peter 3:1 – 2.

Day Two | Passover: Forever Linked to God's Redemptive Story

The Very Words of God

Observe the month of Abib and celebrate the Passover of the LORD your God, because in the month of Abib he brought you out of Egypt by night.

Deuteronomy 16:1

Bible Discovery

Passover During the Time of Jesus

Try to imagine how the ancient Hebrew slaves felt when God revealed that he would send a final plague that would result in Pharaoh driving them out of Egypt. Imagine how careful they would have been to follow every detail of the ritual God commanded to ensure that the death angel would "pass over" their houses and spare their firstborn!

THE HEBREWS PREPARE FOR THE FIRST PASSOVER.

The Passover certainly marked a new day for the Hebrews. Even their calendar would change, beginning at midnight when the final plague began. God commanded his people to commemorate (remember) his great redemptive acts of that first Passover in every generation from that day forward. Thus the Passover celebration is forever linked to God's redemptive story — from its very beginning to its inclusion in Jesus' fellowship celebration, the Lord's Supper.

1. Which specific actions did God command his people to do in preparation for the angel's "passing over"? (See Exodus 12:1 – 28.)

    How did God want his people to remember this day in the future?

How important is it to God that his people continue to relive and pass on the memory of Passover to future generations? (How many times did he say to celebrate it as a lasting ordinance?)

2. In God's view, "remembering" Passover was not just learning that an historical event occurred. What response and actions did God expect from his people as a result of their remembering? (See Leviticus 11:45; 19:33 – 37; 22:31 – 33.)

DATA FILE

Unleavened Bread

God commanded the Hebrews to eat unleavened bread (in Hebrew, *matsah*) at Passover to commemorate their rapid departure from Egypt. (On Passover night, they had no time to let their bread rise.) Like the bitter herbs that symbolized the Hebrews' bondage and described how the Egyptians treated them, *matsah* is called the "bread of affliction" and is another reminder of the Hebrews' experience in Egypt. So unleavened bread represents slavery and freedom, important aspects of their deliverance.

Over time, the Jewish people came to believe that the fermentation of yeast symbolized moral and spiritual corruption. In her article entitled "The Imagery of Leaven," Lois Tverberg[5] helps us to understand this metaphor. Moistened grain or flour soon acquires a sour taste and begins to mold—a natural decaying process—because yeasts and molds in the air start growing and producing acids. People of biblical times learned that fermented dough made better-tasting bread, so they would save a bit of fermented dough in a cool, dry place, then add it to a fresh batch to speed up fermentation. Apparently this practice is the basis of the biblical image of a life contaminated by disobedience to God (1 Corinthians 5:7–8). Like yeast added to dough, sin causes decay. The original lump of dough—Adam and Eve's sin—has been added to every generation since, corrupting all of us.

So, when preparing for Passover, the Jewish people thoroughly cleaned their homes and utensils to remove all leaven. By Jesus' time, collected leaven was burned to symbolize the family's commitment to be completely free of leaven and to remove any sinful act or attitude from their hearts and lives. Today devout Jews still remove all leaven from their homes before Passover (even boiling china, silverware, pots, and pans!) and eat unleavened *matsah* during Passover.

In keeping with this metaphor, when Jesus held up the unleavened bread during the Last Supper and stated, "This is my body," he was saying that he was fit as a sacrifice because he was free of leaven! He had no blemish (John 1:29; Hebrews 4:14–16) and was not infected with decay, so he would live for eternity! (See Psalm 16:10; 49:9; Acts 13:34–37.)

3. Even as God gave instructions for the first Passover, he commanded the Israelites to observe specific practices during all future Passover festivals. Use the chart below to compare the practices of Jesus and his disciples with those of a typical Passover celebration. The Data File "Passover in the First Century" (pages 196–197) will fill in some details of first-century practices that are not specifically mentioned in the Bible.

	Traditional Passover Celebration	**Celebration of Upper Room Passover—the "Last Supper"**
The location:	Deut. 16:1–8	Luke 22:7–12
The preparation:	Ex. 12:3–10	Mark 14:12–16
The food consumed:	Ex. 12:8	Matt. 26:26–28; John 13:21, 26

DATA FILE

Passover in the First Century

The Passover celebration, as God originally intended, deeply touched the hearts and lives of God's people. During the first century, the Romans' cruel occupation of Judea added significantly to the longing of the Jewish people for the kind of deliverance demonstrated when God freed the Hebrews from Egypt. During Passover, this longing became more passionate and often led to violence against Rome. Even without the political tension, the scene in Jerusalem, where the sacrifices of the Passover lamb had to be made, was unbelievable.

Jerusalem at that time was a city of about 50,000 people. Josephus, a first-century Jewish historian, estimated that more than three million pilgrims[6] made the difficult trek to Jerusalem to celebrate Passover. Even if the actual number was much lower, the city was crowded and bustling with activity. All available lodging in the city and in nearby villages was full.

The Passover, unlike other festivals, required each family to sacrifice a lamb, so every family needed to buy a lamb on the tenth day of the month—and keep it until the fourteenth day! All twenty-four divisions of priests prepared for animal sacrifices and the burning of leaven that had been removed from each home or place where Passover would be celebrated. Beginning at the ninth hour (3:00 p.m.), crowds of people gathered at the temple to sacrifice their Passover lambs. There were so many people that the priests had to conduct the sacrifices in three shifts!

The blood of each lamb was caught in a basin and thrown against the foot of the great altar. The lamb was skinned and its fat and kidneys cut away to be burned on the altar. The lamb was then wrapped in its hide and carried out of the temple courts to wherever the family would roast the whole lamb and celebrate the Passover seder.

The evening seder was held in private homes and rented rooms—all within Jerusalem's walls. Celebrants reclined on cushions as the host guided them through the ritual meal. Before the meal, family members ate bitter herbs and unleavened bread to relive their ancestors' hardships while the host recited the exodus story. When the host recited God's final deliverance in Egypt, the family feasted on lamb and drank wine to recall the joy of God's redemption.

Over time, additional foods and practices became a formal part of the seder. By the first century, *charoseth*, a sweet mixture of chopped nuts, apples, wine, and spices symbolized the mortar that Hebrew slaves used in Egypt. Parsley dipped in salt water reminded participants of the Hebrews' tears. And a hard-boiled egg reminded them of Pharaoh's hard heart. The cups of wine consumed during the seder's four parts became associated with God's four promises in Exodus 6. The practice of reciting the exodus story in response to four questions asked by a younger son became customary. After singing or chanting the first part of the Passover song (the *Hallel*) that includes Psalms 113 – 114, many celebrants ended the celebration with prayer in the temple courts.

Reflection

Those of us who have never participated in a Passover seder may find it difficult to picture a ritual meal where every aspect is designed to create "remembrance" and lead celebrants to relive Passover as if they experienced it themselves. But the more we know and understand about this meal, the better we understand the amazing work of redemption that would unfold after Jesus shared the Passover seder with his disciples in the upper room.

> How might our understanding and appreciation of the sacrifice Jesus made for us be enhanced if we were to focus on the "Lord's Supper" and allow it to be as real and influential in our lives as Passover has been for the Jews?

> What might be some ways you could do this?

For example, what might you do in your family or faith community to recall the bitterness of your slavery to sin as well as the sweetness of God's deliverance through the blood of Jesus — God's Lamb?

Or, what might you do to, in effect, clean the sin out of your life in a way similar to how the Israelites cleaned the leaven out of their houses?

Why do you think it is important for followers of Jesus to not only know about the Passover but to *remember* the Passover and its role in our faith history?

What do we miss out on in our walk of faith if we remain ignorant of the connections between Passover and the redemption Jesus offered us through his sacrificial death on the cross?

Memorize

Obey these instructions as a lasting ordinance for you and your descendants. When you enter the land that the LORD will give you as he promised, observe this ceremony.

Exodus 12:24–25

Day Three | Jesus' Last Passover Supper

The Very Words of God

> *When the hour came, Jesus and his apostles reclined at the table.*
> *And he said to them, "I have eagerly desired to eat this Passover with*
> *you before I suffer. For I tell you, I will not eat it again until it finds*
> *fulfillment in the kingdom of God."*

Luke 22:14 – 16

Bible Discovery

Jesus Uses Passover as a Metaphor to Teach about His Mission

Passover was — and still is — a reminder of God's redeeming love for
his enslaved children. As Jesus, God's only begotten Son, celebrated
the Passover seder with his disciples, he used it as a backdrop to
help them understand and remember his act of redeeming love for
all humanity. The seder in the upper room richly portrayed the
past — Israel's deliverance from Egypt; the present — Jesus' imminent sacrificial death as God's Passover Lamb; and the future — a
festival through which Jesus' followers could relive the redemption
Jesus brought through his sacrificial blood. Consider how Jesus used
the ancient, beloved festival of Passover, which his disciples knew
well, as a metaphor to reveal how God's plan of redemption would
unfold.

1. Before Passover, on the tenth day of the first month, what
    did families do in preparation for the celebration? (See Exo-
    dus 12:1 – 5.)

    What did Jesus do on this day? (See Luke 19:35 – 38; John
    12:12 – 15.)

How did Jesus' presence in Jerusalem on "lamb selection day" fit with his mission and how he already had been identified? (See John 1:29, 36.)

2. When Jesus washed his disciples' feet during the seder, he "took off his outer clothing" (in Greek, *tithemi*) and later "put on his clothes" (in Greek, *lambano*) (John 13:4, 12). Rabbis of Jesus' day often illustrated what they taught by what they did as they taught. How might this illustration have related to what Jesus taught earlier about being willing and having the authority to "lay down" his life (*tithemi*) and "take it up again" (*lambano*)? (See John 10:14 – 18.)

    How did John later express to Jesus' followers the importance of our willingness to lay down our lives for others? (See 1 John 3:16 – 18.)

    How do you think remembering (in the biblical sense) the ultimate sacrifice Jesus made at Passover would help us to do this?

DID YOU KNOW?

Taking in the Scene in the Upper Room

Many of us have questions about what it was like to be in the upper room with Jesus and his disciples. The following descriptions and explanations may add knowledge and understanding that will help you refine that picture.

What was the upper room? The Greek word translated "upper room" (Luke 22:12), *kataluma*, is translated "inn" in Luke 2:7. Probably "guest room" is the closest English translation. First-century homes in Israel typically were one- or two-story compounds — called *insulae* — with rooms arranged around a central courtyard. Three or four generations of extended family members would live in an *insula*, sharing rooms for such functions as eating, sleeping, working, and storage. Even today, such family compounds often have guest rooms for visitors.

Who was the greatest? The Roman triclineum style of seating focused attention on one's status at a banquet. The host (B in the illustration) reclined at the second seat on the left as one entered the center of the triclineum (or, if there was no table, in the horseshoe shape). The most honored guest (A) reclined to the host's right, and the next honored guest (C) reclined to the host's left (behind the host). Thus the disciples' contention over who was the

continued on next page ...

greatest (Luke 22:24–30) may have been caused by their need to determine seating placement during the seder.[7]

Clearly the disciples had not taken Jesus' previous teaching (Luke 14:7–11) to heart. So he once again emphasized that the servant ways of God's kingdom, the kingdom that he came to advance, were not the ways of the world. It seems likely that as a rabbi who taught using words and actions, Jesus demonstrated this truth by washing his disciples' feet (John 13:1–17). How ironic it is that Jesus' disciples argued about their greatness during the meal at which Jesus established a memorial celebration of his sacrifice to redeem undeserving, sinful people.

How did they sit? Artists have portrayed Jesus and his disciples sitting on chairs around or behind a high table, but this was not customary during Jesus' time. Celebrants of a seder reclined (Luke 22:14) on the floor around serving platters or low tables (triclinea). Even though the Jews of Jesus' day were subject to Roman rule, which required servants to stand and the wealthy or noble to recline, they reclined at the seder in recognition of their freedom and status before God.

Who was the disciple Jesus loved? Most scholars believe that John was the disciple Jesus loved who leaned against him during the Passover meal. Tradition holds that he was the youngest disciple, and it is likely that the custom of the youngest celebrant being near the host was practiced at this time.

3. Matthew 26:26 says that during the meal Jesus held up the unleavened bread and said, "Take and eat; this is my body." What would the disciples, who knew that leaven symbolized sin, have realized Jesus was saying about himself?

What evidence is there that Jesus' early followers understood the connection he was making through the Passover ritual between himself and messianic prophecies? (See Acts 13:32 – 37.)

How real and essential to their lives does it appear the good news was, and what did it have to do with the ancient promises God had made?

On the basis of their testimony, to what degree do you think they were remembering and reliving the redemptive acts of Jesus? Explain your answer.

4. As astonishing as it may seem to us, Judas had a place of honor — next to Jesus — at the Last Supper. We don't know if he was there because of his sense of self-importance or if Jesus gave him that place as an expression of love for the one who would betray him.

    a. When and how during the Last Supper did Jesus use his position at the table to reveal his betrayer? (See Matthew 26:23 – 24; Luke 22:21; John 13:26.)

b. What insight does Jesus add regarding his path to the cross and Judas' role in that? (See Matthew 26:24; Luke 22:22.)

5. What did Jesus say when he gave the bread to his disciples (Luke 22:19), and how did it express what he had taught them in Capernaum about himself? (See John 6:35, 48 – 51.)

6. The lambs' blood on the doorframes in ancient Egypt caused the death angel to "pass over" the firstborn in those homes (Exodus 12:12 – 13). What would the shed blood of Jesus accomplish? (See Matthew 26:28; Ephesians 1:7; Colossians 1:19 – 22; Hebrews 9:11 – 15.)

7. What did Jesus' early followers recognize that he established that night in the upper room? (See 1 Corinthians 11:23 – 26.)

8. Which element that was not part of the first Passover seder did Jesus use in the Lord's Supper to help his disciples remember and relive his sacrifice for the forgiveness of sin?

DID YOU KNOW?

Many first-century Jews had strong messianic expectations and believed that God would raise up another Moses—the Messiah—who would come during Passover night and deliver them from the hated Romans. In a sense they were right. The second Moses would begin his great work of redemption at Passover, but it would not be deliverance from the Romans, it would be deliverance from bondage to sin.

Reflection

While celebrating Passover with his disciples, Jesus used ancient seder practices to illustrate his teaching. He gave new meaning to the Passover feast without diminishing the events it had commemorated for more than a thousand years. He dramatically presented himself as the Messiah to whom all elements of the Passover seder pointed. His redemptive work as the Messiah would complete the promises God made to his ancient people.

> While teaching in Capernaum, Jesus taught about the life-giving nature of his sacrifice (John 6:53 – 58). How does participating in the Lord's Supper give you life, power, and strength to walk in God's ways?

> In what way(s) does understanding the meaning of the Passover seder help you to better understand the meaning of what Jesus taught during the "Last Supper"?

What did Jesus want his followers to recall — and do — as a result of eating the bread and drinking the wine of the Lord's Supper, the fellowship meal he established?

As you celebrate the Lord's Supper, what about its symbolism, ritual, or story renews your commitment to faithfully take action in response to what Jesus has done for you?

In what specific ways do you "remember" and respond with action to what Jesus has done for you?

Memorize

Be imitators of God, therefore, as dearly loved children and live a life of love, just as Christ loved us and gave himself up for us as a fragrant offering and sacrifice to God.

Ephesians 5:1 – 2

THINK ABOUT IT

The "Last Supper" as a Passover Seder

Many scholars believe that the "Last Supper" was a Passover seder and cite the following biblical evidences for this position:

- Jesus instructed his disciples to prepare for the Passover within the walled city of Jerusalem, where God had placed his name (Luke 22:7–12; Deuteronomy 16:2, 5–8; 2 Chronicles 3:1), and seder required special preparations including a prepared room.
- The Gospel writers and Jesus called their meal *Passover* (Matthew 26:2, 17–19; Luke 22:7–13, 15).
- By rabbinic law, celebrants reclined at a Passover seder (Luke 22:14).
- Key elements of a seder were present for the upper room meal.
- Jesus is linked to the Passover Lamb killed during Passover (John 1:29, 36; 1 Peter 1:19; Revelation 5:12).
- Jesus and his disciples sang a hymn — quite likely the second Hallel — after the "Last Supper" (Matthew 26:30).

Day Four | God's Four Promises

The Very Words of God

> *Therefore, say to the Israelites: "I am the Lord, and I will bring you out from under the yoke of the Egyptians. I will free you from being slaves to them, and I will redeem you with an outstretched arm and with mighty acts of judgment. I will take you as my own people, and I will be your God. Then you will know that I am the Lord your God, who brought you out from under the yoke of the Egyptians."*
>
> *Exodus 6:6 – 7*

Bible Discovery

The Meaning of the Four Cups of Wine

God gave Moses four promises to proclaim to the enslaved Hebrews (Exodus 6:6 - 7). Before Jesus' time, these promises — and the four

cups of wine from which celebrants drank to symbolize them[8] —
had become the organizing theme of seder practice even though
God's Passover commandments did not mention wine. In using cups
of wine to portray his messianic mission that linked the blood of
Passover lambs to his blood, Jesus created a sacramental experience
for his disciples organized around the themes of a Passover seder.

DATA FILE

The Order of a Passover Seder

God commanded that specific rituals be followed at Passover, and through
the years Jewish tradition added related practices. Although questions exist
concerning some details of first-century Passover seder, let's explore what
customarily happened during this meal.[9]

Preparations:

On the tenth day of Nissan, as a family's final details related to seder food
(bitter herbs, unleavened bread, wine), room furnishings, and leaven removal
were completed, an unblemished lamb was selected. Kept until the day of
the seder, the lamb was slaughtered and then roasted on an outdoor spit to
be eaten that evening.

The Seder Ritual:

1. To formally begin the meal, the host raised the first "cup of blessing,"
   said the prayer of blessing, and recited the first Exodus 6:6 promise:
   "I will bring you out...." Celebrants drank from the first cup, and the
   host recounted the Passover story, focusing on God's first promise.
2. The first hand washing occurred.
3. Celebrants ate bitter herbs.
4. Four questions were asked.
5. The meaning of Passover was explained.
6. Celebrants sang or chanted the first part of the Passover song, the
   Hallel (Psalms 113–114).
7. The host raised and blessed the second "cup of deliverance" and
   recited the second promise: "I will free you...." Celebrants drank from

this cup as the host recited the Hebrews' history from Abraham to Moses to the Sinai covenant.

8. The second hand washing occurred.

9. The host took a large piece of unleavened bread, the "bread of affliction," broke it in half, and shared half with celebrants. They dipped it and relived the hardships in Egypt and talked about God's deliverance.

10. When the host reached the point of God's dramatic deliverance through the final plague, celebrants feasted on lamb.

11. The third hand washing occurred.

12. Grace was said after the meal.

13. The host brought out and blessed the *afikoman*, the remaining piece of unleavened bread, which celebrants ate as the final course. Apparently this was the bread Jesus broke to symbolize his body, which soon would be offered for all humanity.[10]

14. The host raised the third "cup of redemption," gave the blessing, and recited God's third promise: "I will redeem you...." Celebrants drank from this cup. This cup became the sacramental cup of the Lord's Supper, representing Jesus' blood shed for the forgiveness of sins.

15. Celebrants sang or chanted the Second Hallel (Psalms 115–118).

16. The host raised the fourth cup, the "cup of protection," said the blessing, and recited God's fourth promise: "I will take you...." Celebrants drank from this cup, a symbol of God bringing Israel to himself and providing protection over his beloved. Jesus did not drink from this cup during the Last Supper.

17. To end the seder, celebrants sang a hymn.

1. Which four promises did God command Moses to give the ancient Hebrews? (See Exodus 6:1 – 7.)

   Promise 1 (v. 6)

   Promise 2 (v. 6)

Promise 3 (v. 6)

Promise 4 (v. 7)

THINK ABOUT IT

A rabbinic midrash (teaching) suggests that God, in the four promises of Exodus 6:6–7, may have been responding to the Hebrews' thoughts and that the Torah only recorded God's part of the conversation. Although nothing in biblical text substantiates this theory, the following conversation can help us to understand the significance of these promises and illustrate God's redemptive love for his people.

Hebrews: "We are slaves to the powerful Egyptians. We will never be free."

God: "I will bring you out from under the yoke of the Egyptians."

Hebrews: "But once we are free, how will we live? We are slaves by nature and have never learned how to live free. We do not know how to act for we are still slaves at heart. And we are slaves to the Egyptians no less. We will still act like Egyptians."

God: "I will free you from being slaves to them."

Hebrews: "But we have been polluted by our slavery in Egypt. We have worshiped their gods and practiced their disobedient practices. We are an unclean people unworthy of this God."

God: "I will redeem you."

Hebrews: "But what if we go back to Egypt? What if the Egyptians come after us to force us back to slavery?"

God: "I will take you as my own people, and I will be your God."

2. The first cup of wine (*ve'hotvati*) that the host raised to
    begin seder is called the "cup of blessing" or "cup of sanctifi-
    cation." The blessing usually associated with it is "Blessed are
    you Lord our God, Creator of the fruit of the vine." The host
    would then recite the first promise of Exodus 6:6.

    a. What connection did this cup have to Jesus' teaching
        about himself and his disciples in John 15:1, 4 – 8?

    b. What "promise" is inherent in this teaching?

3. Celebrants drank from the second cup of wine (*ve'hitvalti*),
    the "cup of deliverance," after the host repeated the earlier
    blessing. This cup was associated with the second promise
    of Exodus 6:6: "I will free you from being slaves." Because
    this cup is not mentioned in the Gospels, some scholars
    assume that Jesus did not use it in any new teaching. After
    this cup, the host began reading from the Torah, focusing on
    God's deliverance from the time of Abraham to the covenant
    on Mount Sinai. The unleavened bread and the lamb were
    served.

    a. What do you think it would have been like to "feast" on
        the words of God from the Torah about his faithfulness
        in delivering his people as you actually ate the meal that
        symbolized God's great acts of deliverance?

b. What impact would a vivid reliving of that experience have on your passion to walk in God's ways?

THINK ABOUT IT
Jesus' Substitutionary Blood Sacrifice

God permitted his people to atone for their sins through the blood of animals — an animal's life for a person's life (Leviticus 17:11). As a person made a Passover offering, for example, the priest would identify the one for whom the blood (caught in a bowl) and the sacrificial meat (in another bowl) was offered as if to say, "This is [name's] flesh; this is [name's] blood." The offerer then knew that the sacrifice was complete.

Through this practice, God molded a people who understood that their sins demanded punishment but that he would provide a way for forgiveness through the substitution of the blood — one life for another. Then one night, Jesus raised the third cup of redemption. By saying, "This is my body . . . this is my blood," Jesus made it stunningly clear that all the blood that had been poured out earlier had pointed to the ultimate shedding of blood — the giving of one life, that of the Messiah, in substitution for all humanity.[11]

4. Jesus raised the third cup of wine (ve'ga'alti), the "cup of redemption," and blessed it. This cup is linked to the third promise of Exodus 6:6: "I will redeem you."

a. What stunning revelation did Jesus make regarding this cup and his blood? (See Matthew 26:27 – 29; Luke 22:20.)

b. What link was Jesus making between the pouring out of blood for the first Passover and the pouring out of his blood that was yet to come? (See Exodus 12:3 - 7, 12 - 13; Matthew 26:27 - 28.)

c. What would Jesus' blood accomplish that the blood of the Passover lambs could not? (See Matthew 26:28.)

DID YOU KNOW?

In biblical tradition, the redeemer intervenes on behalf of an indebted or enslaved relative, pays a ransom, and gains the person's release. The redeemed person is in a sense forgiven and made clean because of the price the redeemer paid. God redeemed the ancient Hebrews by canceling out their "indebtedness" to Egypt and its gods. In a similar way, Jesus paid the sacrifice to redeem humankind, and cancels out the stain of sin from any person who receives him as Lord and Savior. So, the lambs' blood in Egypt, effective for its intended purpose, ultimately pointed to Jesus' redemptive work.

5. The fourth cup of wine (*ve'lakachti*), the "cup of praise" or "cup of protection," was used to complete the seder ritual. It was associated with the fourth promise, "I will take you ..." (Exodus 6:7), which in biblical language referred to the "taking" of a person in marriage, as in taking a person under one's protective care. So this cup represented the protective love God has for his people that is like the love a husband has for his wife.

a. Jesus refused to drink from the fourth cup, the assuring symbol of God's continuing and protective love. What dangers would he soon face as he took the sins of humanity on himself, thus separating himself from his heavenly Father?

b. What does this reveal about his love for all humanity — his love for you?

Reflection

In keeping with God's command to "remember" the Passover, the Jews added the four cups of wine to the seder ritual. In so doing, they highlighted God's amazing promises of redemption and relationship in Exodus 6:6 – 7. Jesus used the cup and promise of redemption to help introduce the fellowship meal of the new covenant that he instituted during the last Passover seder before his sacrificial death (1 Corinthians 11:23 – 26). Just as God commanded the Hebrews to remember the Passover, Jesus commands his followers to remember the body and blood of his sacrifice.

As Jesus' disciples sipped from the cups of the Passover seder and relived God's promises and his fulfillment of them, they must have become keenly aware of what God had done for them. What do you think they felt and thought when Jesus used the elements of the seder to present himself — his body as the "unleavened bread" and his blood represented in the cup — as the long-awaited Messiah/Redeemer?

To what extent do you think Jesus wants his followers today to share the same type of "reliving" experience that his disciples shared at the Last Supper?

How would your experience of the Lord's Supper be different if, the next time you hold the bread in your hands you think of Jesus in the upper room using it as a metaphor for his sinless body? If you think of the disciples' shock as they realized that the cup of wine represented Jesus' blood that he would pour out for their redemption?

What do you think Jesus meant by, "Do this in remembrance of me"? What does he want us to relive?

How might we reclaim the awesome awareness of what Jesus has done for us and what his sacrifice means for our future?

Memorize

Therefore, say to the Israelites: "I am the Lord, and I will bring you out from under the yoke of the Egyptians. I will free you from being slaves to them, and I will redeem you with an outstretched arm and with mighty acts of judgment. I will take you as my own people, and I will be your God. Then you will know that I am the Lord your God, who brought you out from under the yoke of the Egyptians."

Exodus 6:6 – 7

Day Five | Teach Your Children

The Very Words of God

> *When you enter the land that the* LORD *will give you as he promised,*
> *observe this ceremony. And when your children ask you, "What does*
> *this ceremony mean to you?" then tell them, "It is the Passover sacrifice*
> *to the* LORD, *who passed over the houses of the Israelites in Egypt and*
> *spared our homes when he struck down the Egyptians."*
>
> *Exodus 12:25 – 27*

Bible Discovery

Writing Values on the Hearts of Children

Moses knew that gaining freedom is difficult but sustaining it
throughout history is even harder. To forget the story of the
Hebrews' slavery and their forty-year desert journey to the Promised
Land would be to risk losing sight of who God is and all that he had
taught his people. So the Torah commands parents to use the seder
rituals as opportunities to teach children their identity as God's
people and to help them remember God's mighty acts of deliverance. It was the father's duty to answer his children's questions concerning the Passover celebration.

1. The four questions a child is to ask during the Passover seder
    are found in Exodus 12:25 – 27; 13:5 – 10, 14 – 16; and Deu-
    teronomy 6:20 – 25.[12] Write down the four questions to be
    asked (the question in 13:8 is implied) and how they are to
    be answered. (NOTE: The "Type of Child" will be answered
    in question 3.)

Four Questions	Four Answers	Type of Child

Four Questions	Four Answers	Type of Child

2. When did Moses tell the people to recount their exodus experiences to their children? (See Exodus 12:14, 24 – 27.)

    Why do you think he gave these instructions *before* the events took place and *before* the children who needed to learn about them were born?

3. According to Jewish tradition, each of the four questions listed in the question 1 chart corresponds to a type of son who must celebrate and be taught the meaning of Passover. Try to match the child described in a, b, c, and d to the question he would ask.

    a. The wise child whose question indicates a desire for deeper understanding of Passover's meaning. (See Deuteronomy 6:20 – 25.)

b.   The simple or naïve child who desires to be godly but knows little about the Passover's meaning and asks a basic question. (See Exodus 13:14 – 16.)

c.   The child who does not know how to ask a question, so the parent must anticipate the unasked questions and provide appropriate answers. (See Exodus 13:5 – 10.)

d.   The wicked and rebellious child who asks, "What does this mean to you?" rather than "to us?" The parent responds by including the child in the answer and saying, "The Lord spared *our* homes that night." (See Exodus 12:25 – 27.)

4.   Scholars have noted that four "sons" also asked four questions during the Last Supper.

a.   Who is the wise son, what question did he ask, and how did he answer it? (See John 13:12 – 17.)

b.   Who might be the simple or naïve son who asked two questions? (See John 13:33 – 38.)

    c.   Peter instructed someone else to ask Jesus a question, so who might be the son who didn't know how to ask?[13] (See John 13:21 – 25.)

    d.   Who might be the wicked or rebellious son? (See Matthew 26:20 – 25.)

5.   In addition to teaching our children to remember the mighty acts and faithful love of God that are commemorated during the Passover and the "Last Supper," we also must teach them to look forward to the fulfillment of Jesus' promises.

    a.   What is the great and glorious promise of Jesus? (See John 11:25 – 26.)

    b.   What impact did the fulfillment of that promise have on the women who went to Jesus' tomb, and what were they to do? (See Mark 16:1 – 7.)

    c.   What has the resurrection of Jesus given us? (See 1 Peter 1:3 – 6.)

   d. How can we remember and keep this glorious hope alive
       in our hearts and in the hearts of our children as we
       journey through the "deserts" of our lives?

THINK ABOUT IT
What Is Important for Us to Pass On?

The Egyptians passed on their influential culture through magnificent pyra-
mids and temples. Tourists and scholars still visit those monuments, but the
Egyptian civilization that birthed them is long gone. Massive building projects
do not ensure that a worldview, the values of a culture, will be passed down
to future generations.

In contrast, the values of the relatively small Judaic culture of the ancient
Hebrews remain. Descendants of Hebrew slaves who built some of Egypt's
very monuments at a bitter cost still celebrate Passover and still have a profound impact on human history. And followers of Jesus—a descendant of
those slaves—continue to perpetuate his person and work, in part because
they celebrate the meal of remembrance he established using some of the
Passover seder elements.

Moses realized that writing godly values on the hearts of children will main-
tain a worldview from one generation to the next. He forever shaped the
legacy of the Hebrews and the celebration of Passover by commanding parents (even before the death angel passed over) to answer their children's
Passover questions. From one generation to the next, the Passover story (and
its rich heritage that has shaped the Christian faith), continues to transform
the hearts of God's people.

Reflection

The most lasting way for us to ensure that the knowledge of who God is and what he has accomplished in history continues to be passed on from generation to generation is to instill in our children a deep love of the Word of God and awareness of God's historic and ongoing presence and work in our world. Moses, a prophet who walked with God, understood this. His challenge for the ancient Israelites remains our challenge today: "Teach the children."

Our children also participate in the same great, redemptive story of God. As we teach them to remember, praise, and act in obedience to God because of what he did in Egypt, how much more must we teach them to remember, praise, and act in response to the redemption he provided through Jesus, the Passover Lamb, with whom we will one day live forever!

In light of the four questions asked during Passover, write out four questions you believe will lead children toward a deeper understanding and life-giving "remembrance" of Jesus' Last Supper. Then write out four answers.

Four New Questions	Four New Answers

How do you think we can help children experience and know the living hope that Jesus has provided:

by his sacrificial death that delivers us from bondage to sin?

by his resurrection that promises everlasting life with him?

What regular opportunities can you create to share with your children your passion to live in the freedom from sin that Jesus provides?

How important is it for your children to "catch" this passion and live in obedience to God as a result?

In what ways does your faith community help you to do this?

What specific things would you like to see families and faith communities do to pass on the spiritual legacy God has given us — what we know, believe, and live for — to those who will come after us?

Memorize

Only be careful, and watch yourselves closely so that you do not forget the things your eyes have seen or let them slip from your heart as long as you live. Teach them to your children and to their children after them.... Fix these words of mine in your hearts and minds; tie them as symbols on your hands and bind them on your foreheads. Teach them to your children, talking about them when you sit at home and when you walk along the road, when you lie down and when you get up. Write them on the doorframes of your houses and on your gates.

Deuteronomy 4:9; 11:18–20

THE FIFTH CUP:
OUR WAY OF HOPE

It had been an emotional two weeks for the disciples who gathered together in the upper room to celebrate the Passover seder with Jesus. Barely two weeks earlier, Jesus had raised Lazarus from the dead! That miracle increased opposition from religious leaders but built support among Jewish people who flooded into Jerusalem in anticipation of Passover.

Less than a week previously, the disciples followed Jesus into Jerusalem on the day God had commanded families to choose their lambs for Passover. Then Jesus sent them to obtain a donkey at Bethphage, the village that marked Jerusalem's city limit. As Jesus rode into Jerusalem, crowds of devout Jews recognized the fulfillment of Zechariah's ancient prophecy (Zechariah 9:9) that the Messiah would enter the city on a donkey. They responded with messianic fervor. Waving palm branches that symbolized their nationalistic desires and hatred of Roman oppression, they joyfully accompanied Jesus all the way to the temple!

Yes, tension in Jerusalem had dramatically increased during the previous two weeks. The Romans were on guard against the inevitable Passover attacks by Zealots. The corrupt priestly leaders had challenged and plotted against Jesus for quite awhile. During the days leading up to Passover, confrontations with them had escalated. Jesus opposed the chief priests in the temple courts. He turned over tables and drove merchants out of the Gentile Court — a place for prayer — that had been turned into a marketplace. Then Jesus publicly criticized the conduct of top Jewish leaders and declared that God would take the kingdom from them!

As the disciples gathered in the upper room, perhaps they felt a little relief. If so, it didn't last long. Not long into the seder, Jesus told them that God's judgment on sinners was not far off. Then he revealed that one of *them* would betray him! That meant all of them were in danger. As if that news were not startling enough, Jesus reshaped their understanding of Passover by declaring that the *matzah* and the cup of wine after the meal represented a new covenant in *his* body and blood.

After encouraging them, Jesus revealed that soon he would leave them and they could not go with him. The disciples must have been a somber group as Jesus gently told them to demonstrate their love for him in his absence by obeying his teaching. Then they went out into the moonlit night.

The Gospel writers tell us that Jesus also faced intense struggles that night. Death again stalked in the moonlight as it had on the first "pass-over" in Egypt. This time the blood of the Lamb of God would be required to redeem God's people from the bondage of sin into which they had been born. For this purpose Jesus had entered the world.

Several of Jesus' disciples had seen him, the divine Son of God, in all his glory during the transfiguration. During this night they would see Jesus' humanity fully displayed. This night, the Lamb commanded, "Watch with me," and they would see their Messiah — our Messiah — face his destiny. He would pay the price to redeem all of humanity, and he would lift up the cup of eternal life for all who come to him.

Opening Thoughts (3 minutes)

The Very Words of God

> *It is written: "And he was numbered with the transgressors;" and I tell you that this must be fulfilled in me. Yes, what is written about me is reaching its fulfillment.*
>
>

Luke 22:37

Think About It

At one time or another, many of us face seemingly impossible — even terrifying — situations in which we must choose to press on toward accomplishing our objective or to abandon our mission and take a different path.

When you face such extreme situations, what motivates you to press on? Is it the desire to achieve? The longing for reward or status? A sacrifice of love?

What enables you to take on what seems to be impossible? In what do you trust to help you get through risky or frightening situations? What would you do if you knew you were on your own and that there would be no help?

DVD Notes (29 minutes)

A garden and a gethsemane—a place to stay during Passover

What is a gethsemane?

Leyl Shimmurim—the night of watching

The "fifth cup"—the cup of God's fury

DVD Discussion (6 minutes)

1. For the Jewish people, Passover was (and still is) the focal
    point of God's story of redemption. For generations they had
    celebrated this pivotal night in their history as God's people.
    From their homes in Goshen where they first sacrificed their
    Passover lambs and painted the blood on the doorways to
    Herod's temple in Jerusalem, God's people remembered the
    night of their deliverance.

    On the map on page 229, trace the Israelites' journey and
    note the many places they celebrated Passover — Goshen
    in Egypt; Mount Sinai after the tabernacle was built; dur-

ing their years of desert wandering; on the plains of Jericho after they crossed the Jordan River to possess the Promised Land; the temple Solomon built in Jerusalem; and in Jesus' day, Herod's temple. In all of these places, generations of God's people had remembered the Passover. Each remembrance took them closer to this night of watching when the Passover Lamb would step forward for the sacrifice.

2. Try to put yourself in the disciples' place that Passover night. What might have been your mood and thoughts as you walked through Jerusalem — perhaps to the temple courts to pray, then across the Kidron Valley, past the cemetery, and to the gethsemane in the garden where you were staying?

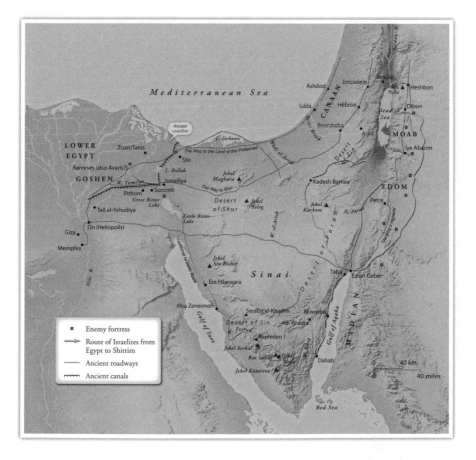

What might have been your hopes and fears?

For what might you have been praising God, and what may have been confusing to you?

3. In what ways does the operation of an olive press — a *gethsemane* — symbolize the pressure Jesus experienced that night as he prayed and waited, feeling the weight of the sins of all humanity and knowing that the death angel would not pass over him?

4. In what way does knowing the tradition of *Leyl Shimmurim* — the night of watching — help you to better understand Jesus' expectations of the disciples whom he asked to keep watch with him?

5. We often acknowledge that Jesus suffered and died because of our sins, but as you watched the video, what new understanding did you gain about what Jesus really did for you?

What does it mean to you that Jesus not only died a tortured death, but that he, God's only begotten Son, faced the full fury of God's wrath so that you would be spared from it?

Small Group Bible Discovery and Discussion (17 minutes)

The Cup of God's Fury

The four symbolic "cups" of the Passover seder (based on the promises of Exodus 6:6 – 7) helped the Jews to recall the miraculous ways by which God kept these promises and delivered his people. Eventually the Jews added another cup to the tradition. Apparently this cup, called "Elijah's cup," originally represented the belief that the prophet Elijah would resolve all questions for which answers could not be found. Over time, Jewish tradition viewed this cup as the one Elijah would drink prior to the Messiah's appearing.

One of those questions focused on the cup associated with God's wrath — the cup that Pharaoh tasted before letting the Hebrews go. Although it is unclear whether or not this "fifth cup" was part of the first-century Passover tradition, it appears that it is the cup Jesus had in mind when he prayed in the garden after the Last Supper for his heavenly Father to "take this cup from me."

1. To the inspired biblical writers, the significance of a "cup" (such as the "fifth cup") was not the cup itself but what was in it. According to Psalms 16:5 – 6 and 23:5 – 6 and Psalm 75:8; Isaiah 51:17 – 20; and Jeremiah 25:15 – 16, 31, what could a cup contain?

Which cup would you want to drink, and why would people be made to drink the other one?

2. Various Bible passages mention God "pouring" the cup of his wrath onto the wicked.

   a. What is that cup like, and what characterizes those on whom he will pour it? (See Psalm 79:6 – 7; Ezekiel 7:3 – 9; Hosea 5:10; Nahum 1:5 – 6; Zephaniah 3:7 – 8; Revelation 14:9 – 11.) Note: If time permits, read all of Revelation 16 also.

   b. How did God demonstrate his judgment against Egypt in the "cup" filled with the wine of his righteous wrath, and what were his purposes in causing Pharaoh to "taste" of this cup? (See Exodus 11:4 – 7; 12:12 – 13, 29 – 30; 14:21 – 28, 31.)

THINK ABOUT IT
He Drank the Cup We Deserve

Our God is righteous and he cannot and will not tolerate sin's corrupting influence — suffering, decay, destruction — in the world he made. His holy anger against any person who brings suffering into the lives of others is frightful to consider. But God is merciful to his creation, so in his plan to redeem people from bondage to sin, he offered his sinless Son, Jesus, to drink the cup of his wrath. The wine of God's anger that would otherwise be "poured out" on sinners would be poured out on Jesus instead.

So the day after the Passover seder, the cup of God's fury against sin was given not to sinful nations, or to brutal Roman overlords, or to scheming religious leaders; it was given to Jesus. The cup over which he agonized on the Mount of Olives was his and his alone to drink. And alone on the cross he drained every drop. He willingly "poured out his life unto death" (Isaiah 53:12) so that God could pour out his love on everyone who receives Jesus as Lord and Savior.

3. After the Passover seder, as he prayed in the garden on the Mount of Olives, Jesus faced the overwhelming reality that in order to provide redemption through his sacrificial blood, he had to drink the cup reserved for sinners — the cup of the holy God's fierce anger against sin. (See Mark 14:32 – 36; Luke 22:42 – 44; Hebrews 5:7 – 9.)

   a. What physical symptom illustrated his anguish, the "pressing" he faced in the agony of his suffering?

   b. Despite the overwhelming human suffering Jesus felt as he faced the path to the cross, he expressed a child-like faith and entrusted himself wholly to the care of his all-powerful Father. In what ways does his testimony of faith speak to you regarding your walk with God?

Faith Lesson (4 minutes)

Each of us deserves the cup of God's wrath, but those of us who have been redeemed and washed clean by the precious blood of Jesus and proclaim him as our Lord and Savior drink a different cup. Instead of drinking from the cup of God's wrath, we drink from the cup of the new covenant that Jesus offered to his followers during the Last Supper (Matthew 26:27 – 29; 1 Corinthians 11:25 – 26). That cup proclaims the death of the Lord Jesus and promises the gift of eternal life (John 3:14 – 15; 6:40; Romans 6:23).

1. Through the video and this study, how has your understanding of and appreciation for what Jesus suffered for you deepened?

   To what extent have you felt the weight of your sin press upon you like a gethsemane presses on crushed olives?

   What do you feel as you envision the oppressive weight of sin Jesus must have felt that night in the garden as he prepared to bear the weight of the sins of the whole world — as he faced the full cup of God's wrath?

   What does it mean to you to have the weight of your sin lifted and removed by God's forgiveness that was made possible by the loving sacrifice of Jesus?

To what extent have you expressed appropriate gratitude to Jesus for what he has done?

2. What have you learned through Jesus' faithfulness in obeying the Father's will and drinking that awful cup that can help you to be faithful in your walk with God?

3. What will you do personally, within your family, and perhaps within your faith community, to remember and relive that Passover seder night — the night of watching — so that you never forget what God did for the Hebrews and what Jesus has done for you?

Closing (1 minute)

Read together John 3:35 – 36: "The Father loves the Son and has placed everything in his hands. Whoever believes in the Son has eternal life, but whoever rejects the Son will not see life, for God's wrath remains on him."

Then pray, confessing to God your wrongdoing and rebellion that has earned for you a deep drink of God's cup of wrath. Thank him for his mercy and for his great story of hope and redemption that continues to unfold. Most important, thank God for sending his beloved Son to drink that awful cup of wrath on your behalf, and with a grateful heart, commit to loving him with all your heart, all your soul, and all your strength.

Memorize

The Father loves the Son and has placed everything in his hands. Whoever believes in the Son has eternal life, but whoever rejects the Son will not see life, for God's wrath remains on him.

John 3:35 – 36

Learning to Walk in the Way of the Lord

In-Depth Personal Study Sessions

Day One | Gardens in God's Plan of Redemption

The Very Words of God

> *When he had finished praying, Jesus left with his disciples and crossed the Kidron Valley. On the other side there was an olive grove, and he and his disciples went into it. Now Judas, who betrayed him, knew the place, because Jesus had often met there with his disciples.*
>
> *John 18:1 – 2*

Bible Discovery

Gardens in the Bible: An Image of Shalom

In the Bible, gardens convey significant meaning because they provide an image of God's *shalom* — his perfect harmony and order.[1] A well-watered and cultivated garden is blessed by God, cared for by his people, and provides everything his people need. During biblical times, even a small garden (and most were a quarter-acre or less) typically provided grapes, olives, possibly figs and pomegranates, and a little grain.

This picture of a blessed relationship between God and his people is why gardens serve as metaphors for the entire biblical story. That great story began with Adam and Eve in a garden, and it will end in the New Jerusalem, which the Bible describes as a garden. But because Adam and Eve rebelled against their holy Creator, thus bringing sin and chaos into God's perfect world, they — and their descendants — could no longer live in intimate relationship with him. They were cast out of God's garden. God sent his Son — Jesus the Messiah — to take the penalty for our sinfulness so that our relationship with him could be restored and we could live with him forever in his eternal garden. As God unfolds his plan to bring his people from the first garden to the last one, it should not surprise us to see Jesus accomplishing his redemptive work in a garden.

1. What had God provided in the garden for the people he had created? (See Genesis 2:8 – 9, 15 – 17; 3:1 – 19.)

    What was his one requirement in the garden?

    How did the people he created respond, and what was the result?

2. The Bible unfolds the story of God's redemptive plan to restore *shalom* to his creation by defeating the power of sin and restoring human beings to intimate relationship with him. Isaiah 58:6 – 11 and Jeremiah 31:11 – 14 give us a glimpse of what that looks like.

    a. Which metaphors describe the people God chose to be his redemptive instruments in bringing *shalom* to our broken world?

    b. What does God's *shalom* look like as it is practiced in the world?

3. What keeps God's restoration, his *shalom*, from being fulfilled through his people, and what then happens to God's "vineyard" and "garden"? (See Isaiah 5:1 – 4, 7; Jeremiah 2:21 – 22.)

DATA FILE

Gardens in Ancient Israel

God promised the ancient Hebrews "a good land — a land with streams and pools of water, with springs flowing in the valleys and hills; a land with wheat and barley, vines and fig trees, pomegranates, olive oil, and honey" (Deuteronomy 8:7 – 8). Even today, Israel — the Promised Land — has fertile land watered by precious rain and springs of water. But it is primarily a land of hills and mountains with few large valleys in between. So during ancient times, the people built terraced gardens on the steep hillsides in order to create land that could be farmed. These terraced gardens were called *ganim*, and each one provided a reasonable quantity of food for the family that cared for

GANIM ON A JUDEAN HILLSIDE

continued on next page . . .

it. Grapevines frequently grew along the edges of the terraces, and small patches of grain grew among the fig and olive trees.

In each family garden, which was an eternal inheritance from God, the people were free to fulfill God's command to care for his creation with all their might. Each *gan* was indeed the place where God — the Creator of all — gave people the responsibility to care for his world. When God gave his people peace, these gardens symbolized the *shalom* they were enjoying because, in effect, the garden of Eden was being restored. And when the Israelites told their children about the garden of Eden, their beautiful terraced gardens provided a metaphorical image their children could understand. When God's people faced difficult times, such as when they were living in exile, they longed for the small gardens and the comfort of having their own vine and fig tree (Micah 4:4).

SOME OF THE ANCIENT TERRACED GARDENS (GANIM) STILL REMAIN ON THE MOUNT OF OLIVES.

The Mount of Olives where Jesus prayed after the Last Supper was covered with *ganim*, a few of which remain to this day. In fact, the mountain was named for the abundant olive trees that grew on its terraced slopes. In one of those gardens, near a gethsemane, perhaps one of the greatest struggles in human history took place. In a pivotal moment, Jesus prayed to be delivered from the cup of God's wrath but also submitted himself to his Father's will.

4. After the Passover seder, where did Jesus and his disciples go and what happened there? (See John 18:1 – 7, 11 – 12; Luke 22:39 – 46.)

What temptation (although that word is not used here) did Jesus face in the garden on the Mount of Olives? (See Matthew 26:36 – 46.)

In what ways was his temptation similar to what Adam and Eve faced in the garden of Eden? (See Genesis 3:1 – 11.)

What effects did their respective decisions to obey or disobey God have on human history and on God's plan for his creation? (See Romans 5:12, 15 – 19; 6:6 – 7; 1 Corinthians 15:20 – 22.)

DID YOU KNOW?

Decisions in a Garden

Adam and Eve's decision to sin in the garden of Eden and Jesus' decision concerning his Father's will in the garden on the Mount of Olives share three crucial aspects. Each decision:

- Dramatically impacted the course of human history and God's plans concerning his creation;
- Related to obeying God;
- Included the temptation to avoid God's difficult path of obedience.

5.   Where was the new tomb in which Jesus was placed after he was crucified, and what event happened there that defeated the power of sin, making it possible for followers of Jesus to receive eternal life? (See John 19:31 – 20:18.)

6.   One day, those who have been redeemed by Jesus, the Son of God, and who acknowledge him as their Lord and King will spend eternity in a garden where God's *shalom* reigns. What will that garden be like? (See Revelation 2:7; 22:1 – 2.)

A GARDEN TOMB

In what ways is that garden like the garden of Eden? (See Genesis 2:8 – 10.)

What do the descriptions of these two gardens say to you about what God has always wanted to provide for the people he created?

Reflection

Biblical gardens symbolize a sacred space where God's abundant provision satisfies human longing, where *shalom* is found, and where death is turned into life. So, the garden on the Mount of Olives was the perfect setting for Jesus to find the strength to obey God's will and remain true to his messianic mission. The garden tomb was the perfect setting for Jesus to live again in triumph over sin and death. The garden is also the perfect setting for God's people to celebrate eternity with him.

In the meantime, God's people have a mission. We are to represent God's "well-watered garden" to the world. We are to obey God with all our heart, all our soul, and all our strength and in so doing display God's *shalom* so that others will come to know him.

> Isaiah 58:6 – 12 tells us how to do this, so take time to thoughtfully read this passage. Then look at your life and your calling to be like a well-watered garden in the lives of others. For each description of God's *shalom* in this passage, write down specific ways you can live it out and fulfill it in your life. Then pray and ask God for the strength to fulfill his will in your life and advance his kingdom on earth.

Memorize

> *The* Lord *will guide you always;*
> *he will satisfy your needs in a sun-scorched land*
> *and will strengthen your frame.*
> *You will be like a well-watered garden,*
> *like a spring whose waters never fail.*
>
> *Isaiah 58:11*

Day Two | A Garden and a Gethsemane

The Very Words of God

When they had sung a hymn, they went out to the Mount of Olives....
Then Jesus went with his disciples to a place called Gethsemane, and
he said to them, "Sit here while I go over there and pray." He took
Peter and the two sons of Zebedee along with him, and he began to be
sorrowful and troubled. Then he said to them, "My soul is overwhelmed
with sorrow to the point of death. Stay here and keep watch with me."

Matthew 26:30, 36 – 38

Bible Discovery

A Symbol of Jesus' Sacrifice

Although the Bible never mentions a "garden of Gethsemane," the
late-night events following the Passover seder did take place in a
"garden" and in "Gethsemane." The location of these events on the
Mount of Olives was not just a random dot on the map. As the names
of places in the Bible often do, the Gethsemane on the Mount of
Olives represented what God was accomplishing that night. It illustrated the impact of what took place that Passover night.

1. Where do the Gospel writers say Jesus and his disciples went
    after celebrating the Passover seder in the upper room? (See
    Matthew 26:30, 36; Mark 14:26, 32; Luke 22:39 – 40; John
    18:1 – 4.)

    What was the general location, and what was it near? (Refer
    to the map of Jerusalem on page 245 to trace Jesus and his
    disciples' steps from the Upper City, where the upper room
    was located, to the general area where they stayed.)

    What does it appear the specific place may have been?

1 Temple Mount
2 Temple
3 Antonia
4 Hasmonaean Palace
5 Herod's Palace
6 Theater
7 First Wall
8 Second Wall
9 David's City
10 Lower City
11 Upper City
12 Business District
13 Garden Gate
14 Towers (Damascus) Gate
15 Kidron Valley
16 Tyropoeon Valley
17 Golden Gate
18 Southern Stairs
19 South Wall
20 Royal Stoa
21 Opening of Entrance Tunnels on Temple Mount
22 Robinson's Arch
23 Barclay's Gate
24 Wilson's Arch & Bridge
25 Warren's Gate
26 Tadi Gate
27 Pool of Bethesda
28 Eastern Gate
29 Double Gates
30 Triple Gates
31 Hinnom Valley
32 Essene Quarter
33 Mansions
34 Entrance to Antonia
35 New City
36 Golgotha (?)
37 Garden Tomb
38 Mount of Olives

OLIVE GROVE ON THE MOUNT OF OLIVES

2. What had Jesus been doing during the days leading up to Passover, and how close to the temple was the place they stayed? (See Luke 21:37.)

FOR GREATER UNDERSTANDING
Where Did Jesus and His Disciples Stay?

After the Passover seder, Jesus and his disciples left Jerusalem, crossed the Kidron Valley, and went to a place on the Mount of Olives where they had been staying. The Mount of Olives is a ridge just east of Jerusalem. During the time of Jesus, part of the ridge was a cemetery and part was terraced with small gardens (*ganim*) that would have had olive trees, grape vines, and a few fig trees. Although the Mount of Olives is no longer the significant olive-producing area it was during the time of Jesus, some of the terraced gardens and olive groves remain to this day, and the cemetery covers a substantial portion of the west-facing slopes.

John said they entered an olive grove on the other side of the Kidron Valley, which would have been on the Mount of Olives (John 18:1–4). The Greek word translated "olive grove," in the NIV is *kepos*, and generally means "a cultivated tract of land" or "garden." John did not name this *kepos* or mention its specific location. Matthew and Mark (Matthew 26:36; Mark 14:32) indicated that they went to a "place called Gethsemane." The Greek word translated "place" means "place" or "property," and not necessarily a garden or farmed plot of land.

The place, Gethsemane, was an oil press. It is likely that it was large or well known, otherwise the writers likely would have called it "a gethsemane." A gethsemane is typically in a cave or building near a cistern containing water. So it is likely that Jesus and his disciples slept in the dry, warm area of an olive press in or near an olive grove or terraced garden on the Mount of Olives. Because a huge number of pilgrims came to Jerusalem to celebrate Passover, lodging was at a premium. An unused olive press (olives are harvested in October and November) would provide shelter from the cold, rainy weather that can occur during Passover. The immediate proximity of Gethsemane on the Mount of Olives to Jerusalem and the temple mount made it an ideal place for Jesus and his small group to stay.

Although there was no place named "garden of Gethsemane" in the biblical accounts, the reference developed because Gospel writers used both a garden and a gethsemane to describe where Jesus and his disciples stayed. In our day, the famous "garden of Gethsemane" is located on the western slope of the Mount of Olives, east of the Old City of Jerusalem. The Church of All Nations (officially known as the Basilica of the Agony) marks the area where, according to tradition, Jesus prayed after the Last Supper. Scholars believe that this twentieth-century church was built on an earlier Crusader chapel, which was built over a fourth-century Byzantine basilica. A small

continued on next page . . .

CHURCH OF ALL NATIONS ON THE MOUNT OF OLIVES

grove of olive trees, believed to date from Jesus' time, is said to be where the disciples slept as Jesus prayed.

Near the church is the "cave of Gethsemane,"[2] which is approximately forty by sixty feet. Believed by a significant scholar to be where Jesus prayed after the seder, it is in a garden and apparently is the site of a large, ancient oil press. Mosaics on its walls indicate that it was a place of prayer for fourth-century followers of Jesus who believed that Jesus' first disciples stayed here before and after the Last Supper.

CAVE OF GETHSEMANE

3. After returning to Gethsemane where he and his disciples
    were staying, how did Jesus prepare himself to face his
    arrest and crucifixion? (See Matthew 26:36 – 44; Luke
    22:39 – 44.)

    What effect did the crushing weight of sin and suffering that
    Jesus would soon bear have on him? (See Luke 22:44.)

    In what sense was the gethsemane a metaphor for the suffer-
    ing Jesus was already beginning to experience?

    NOTE: For a more detailed study of the gethsemane metaphor in
    relationship to Jesus, see *Faith Lessons vol. 4: Death and Resur-*
    rection of the Messiah, session 7, "The Weight of the World."

DID YOU KNOW?

Olives and Olive Oil

Olives were picked when they began to blacken in October and early November. They were transported to an oil press and placed in a basin in which a
large millstone crushed them into pulp. The oil that rose to the surface was
the best oil, the extra virgin oil, and it was skimmed off as an offering to the
Lord. The remaining pulp was placed into woven baskets that were stacked
on top of each other over or in a pit or vat in the floor (usually rock). Stone
weights or a large stone pillar then pressed the pulp to release more oil.

continued on next page . . .

In Hebrew, *gat* refers to any place where something is pressed to make wine, perfume, or oil. The Hebrew word used to describe types of oil or offerings of various oils is *shemanim*. So, the word *gethsemane* comes from the Hebrew word *gat-shemanim*, meaning an oils press.[3]

During Jesus' time, olives were the most significant agricultural crop in Israel. Olives and the oil they produced were used for food, lighting, lubrication, health care, and even ceremonial purposes such as offerings and the anointing of leaders. God frequently used images of the olive tree, its fruit, and its oil to portray himself, his blessing, and his Messiah.

4. Even as Jesus faced his darkest hour, what image of God's *shalom* came to him in the garden? (See Luke 22:43.)

When had this happened before? (See Matthew 4:11; Mark 1:13.)

What insight does this give you into why Jesus repeatedly asked his disciples to pray that they would not fall into temptation? (See Matthew 26:41; Mark 14:38; Luke 22:40.)

Do you think Jesus was being tempted as he prayed in anguish in the garden near Gethsemane? If so, what was he being tempted to do?

Reflection

In the imagery of the Bible, a garden represents God's blessing. So there is a subtle irony in the fact that Jesus faced the painful anguish of his "gethsemane" in a garden. Amidst olive trees and probably grape vines and fig trees that symbolized not only God's blessing but the fruitfulness of God's people in fulfilling his plan of redemption, Jesus faithfully walked the painful path toward the cross.

In what way(s) did the place where Jesus prayed illustrate the intense suffering that he experienced while walking the path toward the cross in obedience to his heavenly Father?

In what ways did the place also illustrate the hope of redemption?

How does the distinction between a garden and a gethsemane help you to better understand the awful price Jesus paid for your sin and why he was willing to do it?

In what ways does the reality of Jesus' suffering, set against the backdrop of a garden — the picture of God's *shalom* — encourage you during times of suffering and struggle in your walk with God?

Memorize

He himself bore our sins in his body on the tree, so that we might die to sins and live for righteousness; by his wounds you have been healed.

1 Peter 2:24

Day Three | What Were the Disciples Thinking?

The Very Words of God

All this I have spoken while still with you. But the Counselor, the Holy Spirit, whom the Father will send in my name, will teach you all things and will remind you of everything I have said to you. Peace I leave with you; my peace I give you.... Do not let your hearts be troubled and do not be afraid.

John 14:25 – 27

Bible Discovery

Making Sense Out of Unsettling Events

When people today study the "Last Supper," they typically focus on Jesus' teachings, his redemptive sacrifice, his washing the disciples' feet, and Judas' betrayal. Of course, Jesus has taught us a great deal about walking with God through these events. But there's another side of the story that we often overlook: the impact Jesus' last days had on his disciples.

Life with their rabbi was about to change dramatically. Perhaps the disciples sensed it. The danger they faced for being his followers seemed to be increasing. Opposition to Jesus by temple authorities seemed to be intensifying at the same time his popularity was growing among the people. And Jesus was saying things about the future that they simply did not understand. What was happening, and what did it all mean?

1. What were the disciples feeling in response to the new things Jesus was teaching and the events of their week in Jerusalem? (See John 13:21 - 22; 16:17 - 18.)

    What kinds of questions did they have for Jesus? (See John 13:23 - 25, 36 - 37; 14:5 - 8.)

    What reassuring words did he have for them? (See John 14:1; 16:33.)

2. How did the crowd of people, Jesus' disciples, and the Pharisees respond when Jesus entered Jerusalem on a donkey less than a week before Passover? (See John 12:12 - 19.)

3. From the temple mount, anyone who had been watching could have seen the procession hailing Jesus as king as it

headed down the Mount of Olives from Bethany, crossed the Kidron Valley, and entered the temple. What do you think Jesus' disciples expected would happen after Jesus overturned merchants' tables in the temple? After he began healing people? After the chief priests and teachers of the law confronted him? (See Matthew 21:10 - 17.)

What had Jesus warned them about before they went to Jerusalem? (See Matthew 16:21; 20:17 - 19.)

Do you think the disciples may have been relieved to stay in Bethany that night rather than in Jerusalem? Why or why not? (See Matthew 21:17.)

4. Review some of Jesus' last actions and teachings at the last Passover seder he celebrated with his disciples and consider what the disciples may have thought or felt in response.

    a. When Jesus washed their feet? (See John 13:2 - 17.)

    b. When Jesus told them Judas would betray him? (See Matthew 26:20 - 25; John 13:18 - 28.)

c. When Jesus linked himself to the unleavened bread and the cup (Matthew 26:26 – 29), particularly in light of his earlier teaching in Capernaum? (See John 6:53 – 58.)

5. What did Jesus reveal during and immediately after the Passover seder that helped his disciples make sense of what had been happening, what would happen, and how they were to continue to follow him after he was gone? (See John 13:36; 14:11 – 21, 23 – 27; 15:10 – 13, 18 – 21, 26 – 27; 16:1 – 4.)

Reflection

It is amazing how quickly Jesus' disciples were able to make sense of all that happened during Passover week. What happened to their beloved Jesus was shocking, devastating, and terrifying. When Jesus died and lived again, his disciples had to choose whom they would serve and the personal price they were willing pay to love him and to continue obeying his commands. Jesus had warned them that people would hate and persecute them for following him but that he would be with them and would send help for them.

Perhaps some of that help came through the hymn they sang together at the end of Passover. Although the Gospel writers do not tell us which hymn Jesus and his disciples sang that evening (Matthew 26:30), Passover celebrants typically sang or chanted the final hymn (Hallel) using Psalms 115 – 118.

So imagine that you were a disciple of Jesus during that last Passover. Write down how these psalms would give you perspective on the events you were witnessing, how they would encourage you to stand by your commitment to obey Jesus' commands, how they would help you to faithfully endure whatever was ahead.

Psalm	What You May Have Felt/Thought
115:1	
115:11	
115:15–18	
116:1–6	
116:13–15, 18–19	
118:5–14	
118:17–19	
118:22–26	
118:28–29	

Memorize

I have told you these things, so that in me you may have peace. In this world you will have trouble. But take heart! I have overcome the world.

John 16:33

Day Four | "Keep Watch with Me"

The Very Words of God

> *Because the LORD kept vigil that night to bring them out of Egypt, on this night all the Israelites are to keep vigil to honor the LORD for the generations to come.*

Exodus 12:42

Bible Discovery

Leyl Shimmurim, the Night of Watching

God commanded that the night following the seder was to be a night of watching. Passover celebrants were to watch and wait in anticipation of God's deliverance. They would see how he watched over them. God's command was not only for that first Passover night; they were to remember what happened that night and to keep watching ... for all generations (forever)!

So in Jesus' time, the Jews were to watch in order to *remember* God's past faithfulness and redemption in Egypt. They also were to watch because God had not yet completed his redemption. He had promised to provide more deliverance, more protection, more of his "watch" over Israel — through his Son, the Messiah! As they vigilantly watched and waited for God's redemption that night after the Passover seder, few Jews realized that the Messiah, whose imminent death and resurrection would advance God's plan to restore *shalom* to all things, was right near them — in Gethsemane!

That night, Jesus the Messiah walked through the city of Jerusalem, crossed the Kidron Valley, and entered a garden or olive grove where there was a gethsemane. He asked three of his disciples to watch and pray with him, then stepped away by himself and, in anticipation of the deliverance that was to come, poured out his heart to God. Not long afterward, he was arrested, and on the very day that his people were watching and waiting for their Redeemer, he offered himself as the sacrifice for all humankind! In order to better understand what really occurred that night, consider again the ancient "pass-over" and *remember* what God did that night in Egypt.

1. The ancient Hebrews placed lambs' blood on their doorposts
   in order to protect their firstborn from God's terrifying final
   plague. What did God do that night — and what did he command his people to do during every night after Passover "for
   the generations to come"? (See Exodus 12:42.)

2. How vigilant was God in "watching" over the Hebrews — in
   providing deliverance and protection for his people from the
   time they left Egypt until they stood on the far bank of the
   Red Sea? (See Exodus 13:21 – 22; 14:19, 24.)

   To what extent does God's "watching" involve active participation as opposed to simply observation?

   In what ways does God's example of "watching" help you to
   better understand his command for his people to "watch" for
   his deliverance?

   Do you think God wants your participation as well as observation? Why or why not?

3. After the seder, what did Jesus command the three disciples to do? (See Mark 14:34, 37 – 41, 50; Luke 22:40.)

In light of God's command in Exodus 12:42, given in anticipation of the Hebrews' deliverance from Egypt, what would the disciples be watching for that night?

In light of Jesus' role in God's plan of redemption, which he had told his disciples about, what do you think Jesus wanted them to be praying about and watching for? Do you think the disciples "got it"? Why or why not?

What insights do Matthew 26:41; Hebrews 2:17 – 18; and 4:15 add into why Jesus and his disciples needed to watch and pray that night?

POINT TO PONDER
Another Time of Temptation?

Jesus emphasized the need for his disciples to watch and pray because of temptation. And because he was fully human, Jesus likely was tempted that night to escape from drinking the "fifth cup" of God's wrath. His prayer, "May

continued on next page . . .

this cup be taken from me" and "not as I will but as you will" suggests that he desired a different path from the one before him. Yet if he was tempted to choose a path other than the cross, he resisted the temptation just as strongly as he had in the desert years earlier and submitted himself to his Father's will. After praying, he stood up to face his betrayer, his enemies, and the cross.

His disciples, on the other hand, were "exhausted from sorrow" (Luke 22:45). The events in Jerusalem, the shock of Judas' betrayal of Jesus, the things Jesus had said during the Passover seder had left them mentally, emotionally, and physically exhausted. Even though Jesus had asked them to keep watch and pray, "so that you will not fall into temptation," they fell asleep. That night they failed to watch vigilantly for God's deliverance.

When the soldiers arrived to arrest Jesus, the disciples faced the temptation to choose a path other than the one of God's choosing, and they fled into the night (Matthew 26:56). Yet God's story of redemption continues. He isn't finished! There is more protection and more deliverance to come. So the disciples' response should help us to remember, to watch, and to pray so that we will be faithful to fulfill our part in God's redemption story.

4. On the Passover night when Jesus was arrested, Jews throughout Jerusalem watched, *remembering* how God had watched over and delivered their ancestors in Egypt. They were also watching for their deliverance.

    a. For what redemptive event were first-century Jews vigilantly waiting and watching at the same time Jesus was praying in Gethsemane? (See Isaiah 53:2 – 7; Micah 5:2.)

    b. We know that in addition to Jesus' disciples, other Jews had faithfully watched and recognized that God's promise was fulfilled, that the Messiah, his deliverer, had come. Which of those showed by his actions that he had been watching, that he was willing to be not only an

> observer but a participant in God's redemption story?
> (See Mark 15:43; Luke 23:50 – 53; John 19:38 – 40.)

Reflection

Our "Passover" has come. Hours after the Passover meal, Jesus the Lamb of God shed his blood to provide deliverance for all people (John 3:16). As the blood of the Passover lambs covered the doorposts of the Hebrews in Egypt and protected them from the angel of death, Jesus' blood covers the doorposts of our lives and protects us from the death we deserve because of our sin. Like the Hebrews before us, we must continue to watch. God's great work of redemption has not run its full course. The Messiah will come again to restore God's *shalom* forever.

Keeping in mind the idea of watching for God's next move in his unfolding plan of redemption, read and reflect on Psalm 121:1 – 8. Jewish people, even to this day, treasure this passage as a description of God's watching over his people as they watch and wait according to his command:

> *I lift up my eyes to the hills —*
> > *where does my help come from?*
> *My help comes from the LORD,*
> > *the Maker of heaven and earth.*
> *He will not let your foot slip —*
> > *he who watches over you will not slumber;*
> *indeed, he who watches over Israel*
> > *will neither slumber nor sleep.*
> *The LORD watches over you —*
> > *the LORD is your shade at your right hand;*
> *the sun will not harm you by day,*
> > *nor the moon by night.*
> *The LORD will keep you from all harm —*
> > *he will watch over your life;*
> *the LORD will watch over your coming and going*
> > *both now and forevermore.*

> *Psalm 121:1 – 8*

How would you describe God's vigilance in watching over his people?

What comfort does his watching provide for you during your painful struggles?

In what ways is his watching an example of how vigilant your watching needs to be?

How faithful are you in remembering the sacrifice Jesus made to deliver you from the penalty of sin?

Is it any less important for you to remember Jesus' sacrifice than it was for the Hebrews and their descendants to remember Passover? Why or why not?

What specific things can you do to cultivate a deeper sense of "watching and waiting" in anticipation of what God will do in your life, your faith community, and your world as his great work of redemption continues to unfold?

Day Five | "Take This Cup from Me"

The Very Words of God

During the days of Jesus' life on earth, he offered up prayers and petitions with loud cries and tears to the one who could save him from death, and he was heard because of his reverent submission. Although he was a son, he learned obedience from what he suffered and, once made perfect, he became the source of eternal salvation for all who obey him.

Hebrews 5:7 – 9

Bible Discovery

Love the Lord Your God with All Your Heart, Soul, and Strength

After the Passover seder, Jesus and his disciples went to Gethsemane on the Mount of Olives where they were staying. There, Jesus was overcome by the agonizing horror and weight of what his messianic mission required of him. In the silvery darkness of a full moon, Jesus fell on his face before God and prayed for his Father to take that awful cup away. But he also was willing to drink the cup if that was his Father's will.

Centuries later, we are amazed by the depth of his suffering. We marvel at his deep commitment to obedience. Yes, he was the sinless Son of God because only the Son of God could take on such a mission. Yet his humanity is undeniable. That night, in the garden, we see the fullness of his humanity. We see Jesus, the sinless Messiah, as one of us. He was in anguish over the path that lay ahead of him, yet he was faithful to obey the will of his Father no matter where it led. Even as the horror of his suffering loomed before him, he lived to love the Lord his God with all his heart, all his soul, and all his strength.

1. Jesus knew the night of watching was coming. It was the reason he had come. During the Last Supper, what did Jesus say to his disciples that revealed his awareness that he would have to pour out his blood as a sacrifice on behalf of sinners — "transgressors"? (See Isaiah 53:12; Luke 22:36 – 37.)

2. During the final hours before his arrest, Jesus suddenly became overwhelmed by the dreadful reality that he would have to drink the cup of God's fierce anger against sin and ungodliness. Take a closer look at what Jesus, a Jewish man who loved God and sought to live by his every word, experienced that night.[4] (See Matthew 26:36 – 39; Mark 14:32 – 36; Luke 22:42 – 44; Hebrews 5:7 – 8.)

   a. Where did Jesus go and what did he do as he struggled to face the horror of what the next hours would require of him?

   b. To whom did Jesus turn to find strength for what lay ahead, and what help did he receive?

   c. What did Jesus plead for God to do concerning the "cup" of God's wrath?

    d.   What deep, intense emotions did Jesus experience as he faced and accepted the suffering that obeying the Father's will would require?

    e.   What physical symptom demonstrated his anguish and the agony of bearing the weight of all humanity's sins?

    f.   Even during this time of overwhelming distress, in what ways did Jesus continue to love, trust, and obey his heavenly Father?

FOR GREATER UNDERSTANDING
The Depth of Jesus' Distress

Imagine the deep emotions that Jesus felt as the weight of the world's sins began to press down on him. Soon God would "pour out" the cup of his anger like fire (Nahum 1:6) on Jesus, who literally would pour out his blood for humankind. Translators have struggled to find in modern languages appropriate words to capture the emotional intensity and force of *ekthambeo* and *ademaneo,* the words used to describe Jesus' emotional state in the oldest Greek manuscripts of Mark 14:33: "he began to be deeply distressed and troubled ... overwhelmed with sorrow to the point of death."

- *Ekthambeo* (translated "deeply distressed," "troubled," or "greatly distressed") conveys the idea of sudden amazement or shock. It connotes "terrified surprise"[5] or "dawning awareness that produces horror."[6] In the garden that night Jesus, in his human nature, became suddenly and shockingly overwhelmed by something that caused him to be filled with dread.
- *Ademaneo* (translated "troubled," "very heavy," "distressed," "anguished," or "depressed") suggests an emotion so strong as to create agitation and confusion.

In addition to the emotional anguish Jesus felt as the reality of the brutal suffering he would soon have to endure set in, "his sweat was like drops of blood" (Luke 22:44). This extreme physical condition, called *hemohidrosis*, occurs when immense emotional stress causes the capillaries in the hands, arms, and forehead to rupture, causing bloody sweat.[7] The few reported examples of this condition have been found in healthy individuals who knew that their deaths were imminent and yet could not prevent them.

3. When Peter made a feeble attempt to fight off with his sword the crowd that came to arrest Jesus, what did Jesus say concerning his submission to his Father's will? (See John 18:11.)

From Jesus' response, what do you think was the alternate choice if he had not chosen the cup?

Do you think he had considered making that choice? Why or why not?

4. What were Jesus' last words on the cross? (See Matthew 27:45 – 50; John 19:28 – 30.)

In what ways does the vinegar illustrate the bitterness of the cup Jesus had to drink?

When, in relationship to fulfilling the Father's will and draining the last drop of the cup, did Jesus die, and what does this say to you about the depth of his love (obedience) for God?

5. Try as we might, we cannot fully understand the mystery
    of Jesus' incarnation — God becoming flesh, one of us. Yet
    the Bible emphasizes that Jesus was fully human and fully
    divine. How these two natures existed in one person is a
    delightful divine mystery, and the Bible affirms them both.
    Consider how the following examples from the text reveal
    his fully human and fully divine nature.

Text	The Humanity of Jesus
Luke 2:52	
John 1:14	
1 Cor. 15:21 – 22	
Heb. 2:14 – 18	
Heb. 4:14 – 16	

Text	The Divinity of Jesus
Matt. 11:27 – 30	
Matt. 14:25 – 33	
Matt. 16:13 – 17	
John 9:24 – 38	
John 10:30 – 38	

Reflection

The story of Jesus' suffering draws us to him. His anguish reminds
us of the painful struggles we face as we seek to walk in God's ways.
Although the reason for his agony far transcends any of our experiences, we can sense his empathetic understanding of our struggles.
He knew them, too. He was one of us.

The first humans chose their own way rather than the path of obedience to their Creator. Jesus — the "second Adam" — faced the same choice, and he lived a life of complete submission to the will of his Father, even when the path of obedience led to the cross. His choice gives us hope because we, too, have to choose between our own path and the path of obedience to God's every command. As Jesus' disciples, we must imitate him. Although we may at times plead with painfully honest cries and tears, "May this be taken away," we also must follow Jesus' example and learn to say, "Not as I will, but as you will."

That is the choice that brings hope — not just for us, but for all of humanity. When we obey the will of the Father, we become participants in his unfolding story of redemption. The path of obedience, even when it leads to the cross, is the path that leads to God's *shalom*. It is the path that Jesus walked so that we might have eternal life, and it is the path he desires us to walk so that others will come to know him.

> What does Jesus' night of watching and his faithful obedience to God, even though it required death on the cross, mean to you? How does it touch the depth of your soul? How does it influence your daily life?

Take some time to write, in your own words, what Jesus' path to the cross means to you. Read it often so that you will *remember* your deliverance as God commands. As the following personal testimony demonstrates, it will make a difference in your life.

> The pictures in God's biblical story are emotionally powerful and rich. For me, none have greater impact than Jesus, face down in the presence of his Father, picturing in his mind a cup filled with God's anger against me and pleading in anguish for the cup to be taken away. That cup would have been reserved for me. I would have had to drink it. Instead,

willingly submitting to his Father's purpose, Jesus went to the cross and drank that cup for me.

I cannot think of a more powerful, humbling story than this one. And I cannot imagine other people not wanting to believe in this Messiah who drank this cup for them, too. The gratitude I feel leads to a burning desire to obey him as an expression of my love for what he has done, to be passionately committed to "walk as Jesus walked," living every day devoted to the path God calls me to walk.

This path, which is not easy, can only be walked if the Spirit enables us, the text guides and directs us, and a faithful community supports us — a community that is awake and in prayer. Walking this path involves commitment of the heart, soul, and mind to live every day in passionate gratitude for the cup Jesus willingly drank on my behalf.

Ray Vander Laan

Memorize

Your attitude should be the same as that of Christ Jesus: Who, being in very nature God, did not consider equality with God something to be grasped, but made himself nothing, taking the very nature of a servant, being made in human likeness. And being found in appearance as a man, he humbled himself and became obedient to death — even death on a cross!

Therefore God exalted him to the highest place and gave him the name that is above every name, that at the name of Jesus every knee should bow, in heaven and on earth and under the earth, and every tongue confess that Jesus Christ is Lord, to the glory of God the Father.

Philippians 2:5 – 11

NOTES

Introduction

1. Jesus' death (as the Lamb of God) was apparently on Passover; he was buried as the Unleavened Bread festival began, and was raised at the beginning of First Fruit.

2. Since we hold the Bible to be God's revealed word, we reject the arguments of many scholars who do not believe the exodus occurred or at least did not occur as the Bible describes it.

3. A defense of this position can be found in *The Moody Atlas of Bible Lands* by Barry J. Beitzel (Chicago: Moody Press, 1985).

4. A defense of this position can be found in *Exploring Exodus: The Origins of Biblical Israel* by Nahum M. Sarna (New York: Schocken Books, 1996).

Session One

1. For a more in-depth study of the Essenes, the Qumran community, and the Dead Sea Scrolls, see *Faith Lessons vol. 3: Life and Ministry of the Messiah*, Session 3, "The Time Had Fully Come."

2. The divine name, Jahweh, is written as four dots in this scroll.

3. This scroll is designated as 1QS, which stands for Qumran Cave 1, Serekh ha-Yachad.

4. It is important to note that John would not have been known as "the Baptist" by his contemporaries. "Baptism" does not come from a Hebrew word, and at the time John's practice was called "immersing." It was an indication of repentance, not the practice people today recognize as Christian baptism.

Session Two

1. John, the son of Zechariah and Elizabeth, was not likely to have been known as "the Baptist" by his contemporaries. They would have referred to John's practice as "immersing," not baptism. A more culturally accurate description would be "John the Immerser." This distinction also makes it less likely that modern readers of the Christian text will assume that John was practicing some form of "Christian baptism," which is quite different in its symbolic meaning.

2. Rainer Riesner, "Bethany beyond the Jordan," in *Anchor Bible Dictionary*. See also Rami Arav and Richard A. Freund, *Bethsaida: A City by the North Shore of the Sea of Galilee*, vol. 2 (Kirksville, Mo.: Truman State University Press, 1999), 373 – 396. The chapter entitled "Bethsaida and a First-Century House Church" has an excellent discussion of Bethany beyond the Jordan and the location where John baptized. See also Bargil Pixner, *With Jesus Through Galilee* (Rosh Pina: Israel Corazin Publishing, 1992).

3. Hershel Shanks, ed., "The Dead Sea Scrolls and Christianity," *Understanding the Dead Sea Scrolls* (New York: Vintage Books, New York, 1993), sect. 5.

4. Josephus, *Jewish War* 2:120.

5. *Jewish War* (2:567)

6. It is likely the soldiers were Jewish soldiers in Herod's army and not Roman troops. Josephus tells us that Herod's soldiers liked John. Besides, there is no hint of any invitation to Gentiles or to the larger world in John's preaching. That would be a significant part of the message of the one to whom he pointed.

7. Alfred Edersheim, *The Temple and Its Services* (London: James Clarke, 1959). An excellent description of the temple and its ritual is presented in this text.

8. If you were to ask an Orthodox rabbi when and where the kingdom of heaven first appeared in the Bible, he would likely say when the Hebrews praised their God who is reigning forever and ever. Clearly the Bible, from Genesis 1 forward, describes God as the sovereign Creator over all creation. As recorded in Exodus, God redeemed a particular covenant people with great power and they acknowledged his lordship and reign. Individually and as a community they needed to enthrone him as the King of their lives. God desired them to become a living example of his reign and its *shalom* to all nations.

9. *Manual of Discipline*, 5:13 – 15

10. *Antiquities* 18.5.2.

Session Three

1. The Greek word translated "made his dwelling" is the same word translated "tent" or "tabernacle," so the text literally states that Jesus "tabernacled" among us.

2. The Jews interpreted this passage as a prediction that a prophet like Moses would be the Messiah.

3. Jerome Murphy-O'Connor, "Triumph Over Temptation," *Biblical Archaeology Review* (August 1999). This article is an exceptional study of Jesus' temptations as recorded by Matthew. Although I do not agree with all of Murphy-O'Connor's conclusions, I (Ray Vander Laan) am indebted to him for many of his insights.

4. I have experienced the same reaction from religious Jewish people today. When they hear Matthew (even in English) they immediately recognize the background from Deuteronomy, even without the direct quote from verse 3.

Session Four

1. Due to John's description of the meal, especially John 18:28 and 19:14, some scholars believe that Jesus ate the meal just before Passover began (hence the meal was not technically a seder) or that there were two different ways of reckoning time. I (Ray Vander Laan) personally believe that the Last Supper was indeed a seder and that John's account can be harmonized with the others. A detailed discussion of this issue is beyond the scope of this study, but many excellent sources investigate this interesting issue, including the following: *Our Father Abraham: Jewish Roots of the Christian Faith* by Marvin Wilson, *Jesus' Last Night with His Disciples* by James W. Fleming, and *Last Supper and Lord's Supper* by I. Howard Marshall.

2. I am greatly indebted to Lois Tverberg for her work explaining ancient meal customs. See Ann Spangler and Lois Tverberg, *Sitting at the Feet of Rabbi Jesus* (Grand Rapids: Zondervan, 2009), chapter 10.

3. 1 Corinthians 11:24 – 25.

4. A contemporary example of such a reconciliation meal, called a *sulha* in Arabic, can be found at *http://jewsforjesus.org/topics/judaica/jewsgentiles/?y=&a=109&p=*. Ilan Zamir, an Israeli Christian, had killed an Arab family's deaf thirteen-year-old son in a car accident and wanted to seek forgiveness from the family. Many tried to stop him because the Arab culture would have allowed the family to kill him as revenge for their son's death. But he insisted. An Arab pastor helped to arrange a *sulha*. At this meal Zamir apologized and offered gifts for what he had (unintentionally) done. The family would not accept the gifts, but when the father of the dead boy began the meal, it demonstrated to everyone his forgiveness. The family then said to Zamir, "Know, O my brother, that you are in place of this son who has died. You have a family and a home somewhere else, but know that here is your second home." What a miracle of grace and mercy!

5. *Sitting at the Feet of Rabbi Jesus*, chapter 8. See also "The Imagery of Leaven" by Tverberg at *www.egrc.net/*.

6. Josephus, *Jewish War*, 2.14.3; 6.9.3.

7. See Alfred Edersheim's *The Life and Times of Jesus the Messiah*, book 5, chapter 10. Edersheim's work, while not having access to the archaeologicial discoveries of the last fifty years, is an exceptional study of the cultural context of Jesus' ministry.

8. The practice of having four cups to correspond to the four promises God made to Israel and kept during the first Passover is attested in Jesus' time although it had not been formalized. It is likely that early in the practice there was a common cup (or the host had four cups) from which all drank four times. Jesus seemed to indicate this common cup when he indicated it symbolized his blood (1 Corinthians 11:26). Only later did the custom evolve of providing four cups for each celebrant.

9. You are encouraged to read all four Gospel accounts carefully before proceeding in this study: Matthew 26:17 – 30; Mark 14:12 – 26; Luke 22:7 – 30; John 13:1 – 17.

10. David Daube, a Jewish biblical and legal scholar at Oxford University, has demonstrated that the practice of *afikomen* occurred during Jesus' time and had messianic overtones because it portrayed a "coming one" who would bring a greater future. Possibly this practice provided the background for Jesus' use of bread to represent his body. He used an element of seder the disciples already understood as having messianic implications and claimed them for himself. The article can be seen at *www.hebrew-streams.org/works/judaism/afikoman.html*. A more detailed treatment is found in David Daube, *The New Testament and Rabbinic Judaism* (London: Athlone Press, University of London, 1956; Peabody, Mass.: Hendrickson, 1994). See also Daube's related study on Passover-New Testament links in "The Earliest Structure of the Gospels," *New Testament Studies 5* (1959): 174 – 187.

11. For further study see Bernhard Lang, "The Eucharist — A Sacrificial Formula Preserved," *Biblical Archaeology Review* (December 1994) and Bruce Chilton, "The Eucharist — Exploring Its Origins" in the same issue. While I have a higher view of Scripture than these authors and do not accept many of the conclusions in these articles, their insights into the temple context of Jesus' words regarding the *matzah* and wine in relationship to his body are very helpful.

12. Deuteronomy 6:20 – 25 does not specifically refer to seder, but because these verses instruct parents in teaching their children about events that seder commemorates, Jews have traditionally

viewed this passage as a command regarding the instruction of children during Passover.

13. The "disciple whom Jesus loved" is believed to be John.

Session Five

1. For a more extensive consideration of Israel's ancient gardens and their crops, please see *Faith Lessons vol. 10: With All Your Heart*, session 6, "A Well-Watered Garden."

2. Joan Taylor, "The Garden of Gethsemane: Not the Place of Jesus' Arrest," *Biblical Archaeology Review* (July/August, 1995), is an excellent review of the archaeological detail of the cave, formerly a gethsemane or olive press.

3. Taylor ("The Garden of Gethsemane: Not the Place of Jesus' Arrest") suggests that the various grades of oil obtained may explain the "oils" press. Others have suggested it may be due to the amount of oil produced.

4. Schalom Ben-Chorin, *Brother Jesus: The Nazarene through Jewish Eyes* (Athens, Ga.: University of Georgia Press, 2001). I (Ray Vander Laan) am indebted to Ben-Chorin, a Jewish scholar, for his deep insight into Jesus' participation in the Jewish culture of his time. This book has a deep appreciation of the nature of Jesus' life and particularly his suffering. The chapters on the Last Supper and Jesus' struggle in Gethsemane are most helpful.

5. Henry Swete, *The Gospel According to St. Mark* (London: Macmillan, 1908).

6. Raymond E. Brown, "The Death of the Messiah: From Gethsemane to the Grave," *Anchor Bible Reference Library* (New York: Doubleday, 1994).

7. William D. Edwards, Wesley J. Gabel, and Floyd E. Hosmer, "On the Physical Death of Jesus," *Journal of the American Medical Association*, vol. 255, no. 11 (March 21, 1986), 1456.

ACKNOWLEDGMENTS

The people of God set out on a journey, a journey from bondage to freedom, a journey to the Promised Land, a place flowing with milk and honey. A simple journcy, really: leave Egypt and walk to the Promised Land. All they had to do was cross the Sinai Desert and they were there. It would not take long; it was only two hundred miles. But God had another route planned. During the forty years that journey took, the Hebrews, concerned about themselves as we all are, became a community — a people who would put the Creator of the universe on display for a broken world.

The production of this study series is also the work of a community of people. Many contributed of their time and their talent to make it possible. Recognizing the work of that unseen community is to me an important confirmation that we have learned the lessons God has been teaching his people for three thousand and more years. It takes a community. These are the people God has used to make this entire series possible.

The Prince Foundation:

The vision of Elsa and Ed Prince — that this project that began in 1993 would enable untold thousands of people around the world to walk in the footsteps of the people of God — has never waned. God continues to use Elsa's commitment to share God's story with our broken world.

Focus on the Family:

Clark Miller — chief strategy officer
Robert Dubberley — vice president, content development
Paul Murphy — manager, video post production
Cami Heaps — associate product marketing manager
Anita Fuglaar — director, global licensing

Carol Eidson — assistant to business affairs director

Brandy Bruce — editor

That the World May Know:

Alison Elders, Lisa Fredricks — administrative assistants

Chris Hayden — research assistant. This series would not have been completed nor would it have the excellence of content it has without his outstanding research effort.

The Image Group and Grooters Productions:

Mark Tanis — executive producer

John Grooters — producer/director

Amanda Cooper — producer

Eric Schrotenboer — composer/associate producer

Mark Chamberblin, Adam Vardy, Jason Longo — cinematography

Dave Lassanke, Trevor Lee — motion graphics

Drew Johnson, Rob Perry — illustrators

Sarah Hogan, Judy Grooters — project coordinators

Ken Esmeir — on-line editor and colorist

Kevin Vanderhorst, Stephen Tanner, Vincent Boileau — post-production technical support

Mark Miller, Joel Newport — music mixers

Keith Hogan, Collin Patrick McMillan — camera assistants

Andrea Beckman, Rich Evenhouse, Scott Tanis, Kristen Mitchell — grips

Shawn Kamerman — production assistant

Marc Wellington — engineer

Juan Rodriguez, Paul Wesselink — production sound

Ed Van Poolen — art direction

Zondervan:

John Raymond — vice president and publisher, curriculum

Robin Phillips — project manager, curriculum

Mark Kemink — marketing director, curriculum

T. J. Rathbun — director, audio/visual production
Tammy Johnson — art director
Ben Fetterley — book interior designer
Greg Clouse — developmental editor
Stephen and Amanda Sorenson — writers

BIBLIOGRAPHY

To learn more about the cultural and geographical background of the Bible, please consult the following resources.

Anderson, Richard. "Luke and the Wicked Tenants." *Journal of Biblical Studies* 1.1.

Arav, Rami and Richard A. Freund. *Bethsaida: A City by the North Shore of the Sea of Galilee, Volume 2.* Kirksville, Mo.: Truman State University Press, 1999, 373 – 396. The chapter entitled "Bethsaida and a First-Century House Church" has an excellent discussion of "Bethany beyond the Jordan" and the location where John baptized.

Barth, Markus. *Rediscovering the Lord's Supper.* Atlanta: John Knox Press, 1988.

Basser, Herbert W. "The Jewish Roots of the Transfiguration." *Biblical Archaeology Review* (June 1998): 30.

Beale, G. K. "An Exegetical and Theological Consideration of the Hardening of Pharaoh's Heart in Exodus 4 – 14 and Romans 9." *Trinity Journal* 5 NS (1984): 129 – 154.

Beitzel, Barry J. *The Moody Atlas of Bible Lands.* Chicago: Moody Press, 1985.

Berlin, Adele, and Marc Zvi Brettler. *Jewish Study Bible.* Philadelphia: Jewish Publication Society and New York: Oxford University Press, 2004.

Bivin, David. *New Light on the Difficult Words of Jesus: Insights from His Jewish Context.* Holland, Mich.: EnGedi Resource Center, 2005. *www.egrc.net.*

Bokser, Baruch M. *The Origins of the Seder.* Los Angeles: University of California Press, 1984.

Borowski, Oded. *Daily Life in Biblical Times.* Atlanta: Society of Biblical Literature, 2003. *www.sbl-site.org.* (Accessed 30 September 2009.)

Bottéro, Jean, Elena Cassin, and Jean Vercoutter, eds. *Near East: The Early Civilizations.* New York: Delacorte Press, 1967.

Brown, Raymond E. *The Death of the Messiah: From Gethsemane to the Grave.* Anchor Bible Reference Library. New York: Doubleday, 1994.

Cernea, Ruth Fredman, *The Passover Seder.* Philadelphia: University of Pennsylvania Press, 1981.

Clements, Ronald, ed. *The World of Ancient Israel: Sociological, Anthropological, and Political Perspectives.* Cambridge: Cambridge University Press, 1991.

Davis, John J. *Moses and the Gods of Egypt: Studies in Exodus.* Grand Rapids: Baker, 1971.

deGeus, C. H. J. "The Importance of Agricultural Terraces." *Palestine Exploration Quarterly* 107 (1975): 65 – 74.

_____. "The Importance of Archaeological Research in the Palestinian Agricultural Terraces with an Excursus on the Hebrew Word *gbi.*" *Palestinian Exploration Quarterly* (PEQ) 107 (1975).

Dickson, Athol. *The Gospel According to Moses: What My Jewish Friends Taught Me about Jesus.* Grand Rapids: Brazos Press, 2003.

Edelstein, Gershon and Shimon Gibson. "Ancient Jerusalem's Rural Food Basket." *Biblical Archaeology Review* 44 (July/August 1981).

Edersheim, Alfred. *The Temple: Its Ministry and Services as They Were at the Time of Jesus Christ.* London: James Clarke & Co., 1959.

_____. *The Life and Times of Jesus the Messiah.* Peabody, Mass.: Hendrickson, 1993.

Elbaum, Leiah. *Plants of the Bible.* Leiah Elbaum, ed. N.p., 2003. *http://natureisrael.com/plants2002.html.* (Accessed 28 September 2009.)

Feeley-Harnik, Gillian. *The Lord's Table: Eucharist and Passover in Early Christianity.* Philadelphia: University of Pennsylvania Press, 1981.

Feiler, Bruce. *Walking the Bible: A Journey by Land through the Five Books of Moses.* New York: HarperCollins, 2002.

Fleming, James W. *Desert Spirituality.* LaGrange, Georgia: Biblical Resources, 2002.

_____. *The Explorations in Antiquity Center.* LaGrange, Georgia: Biblical Resources, 2007.

_____. *Jesus' Last Night with His Disciples.* LaGrange, Georgia: Biblical Resources, 2008.

Fretheim, Terence E. *Exodus: Interpretation, A Bible Commentary for Teaching and Preaching.* Louisville: John Knox Press, 1991.

Friedman, Richard Elliot. *Commentary on the Torah.* San Francisco: Harper, 2001.

Ginzberg, Louis. *An Unknown Jewish Sect.* New York: Jewish Theological Seminary of America, 1976.

Hareuveni, Nogah. *Nature in Our Biblical Heritage.* Kiryat Ono, Israel: Neot Kedumim, 1980.

_____. *Tree and Shrub in Our Biblical Heritage.* Kiryat Ono, Israel: Neot Kedumim, 1980.

Hepper, Nigel F. *Illustrated Encyclopedia of Bible Plants.* Grand Rapids: Baker, 1992.

Hillers, Delbert R. *Covenant: The History of a Biblical Idea.* Baltimore: Johns Hopkins Press, 1969.

Hoffmeier, James K. *Ancient Israel in Sinai.* Oxford: Oxford University Press, 2005.

_____. *Israel in Egypt.* Oxford: Oxford University Press, 1996.

Homan, Michael M. "The Divine Warrior in His Tent." *Biblical Archaeology Review* (December 2000).

Howard, Kevin, and Marvin Rosenthal. *The Feasts of the Lord.* Nashville: Thomas Nelson, 1997.

Jeremias, Joachim, Norman Perrin, translator. *The Eucharistic Words of Jesus,* 3rd ed. Philadelphia: Fortress Press, 1966.

Jordan, Jennifer. "The Wine of Israel and Wine in Biblical Times." Posted 27 October 2006. EzineArticles.com. *www.ezinearticles.com/?The-Wine-of-Israel-and-Wine-in-Biblical-Times&id=340401.* (Accessed 28 September 2009.)

Kitchen, Kenneth A. "The Desert Tabernacle: Pure Fiction or Plausible Account?" *Bible Review* (December 2000).

Kline, Meredith G. *Treaty of the Great King.* Grand Rapids: Eerdmans, 1962.

Khouri, Rami. "Where John Baptized." *Biblical Archaeology Review* (January/February 2005).

Lesko, Barbara and Leonard. "Pharaoh's Workers." *Biblical Archaeology Review,* (January/February 1999).

Lesko, Leonard H., ed. *Pharaoh's Workers.* Ithaca, N.Y.: Cornell University Press, 1994.

Levenson, Jon D. *Creation and the Persistence of Evil.* Princeton, N.J.: Princeton University Press, 1988.

_____. *Sinai and Zion: An Entry into the Jewish Bible.* San Francisco: Harper, 1985.

Levine, Baruch A. *The JPS Torah Commentary: Leviticus.* Philadelphia: Jewish Publication Society, 1991.

Magness, Jodi. *The Archaeology of Qumran and the Dead Sea Scrolls.* Grand Rapids: Eerdmans, 2002.

Maier, Paul L., trans. *Josephus: The Essential Works.* Grand Rapids: Kregel, 1988.

Marshall, I. Howard. *Last Supper and Lord's Supper.* Grand Rapids: Eerdmans, 1981.

Martinez, Florentino Garcia. *The Dead Sea Scrolls Translated: The Qumran Texts in English.* Grand Rapids: Eerdmans, 1996.

Milgrom, Jacob. *The JPS Torah Commentary: Numbers.* Philadelphia: Jewish Publication Society, 1991.

Murphy-O'Connor, Jerome. "Triumph Over Temptation." *Biblical Archaeology Review* (August 1999).

Notley, R. Steven. "Are You the One Who Is to Come?" CD of workshop given at the En-Gedi Resource Center, Holland, Michigan 2002. *www. egrc.net.*

Peterson, Eugene. *Eat This Book.* Grand Rapids: Eerdmans, 2006.

Pixner, Bargil. *With Jesus Through Galilee According to the Fifth Gospel.* Rosh Pina, Israel: Corazin Publishing, 1992.

Pryor, Dwight. *Unveiling the Kingdom of Heaven.* Dayton, Ohio: Center for Judaic Christian Studies, 2008.

Rainey, Anson F., and R. Steven Notley. *The Sacred Bridge: Carta's Atlas of the Biblical World.* Jerusalem Israel: Carta, 2006.

Riskin, Shlomo. *Torah Lights: Genesis Confronts Life, Love and Family.* Jerusalem: Urim Publications, 2005.

_____. *Torah Lights: Exodus Defines the Birth of a Nation.* Jerusalem: Urim Publications, 2005.

Rosen, Ceil and Moishe. *Christ in the Passover.* Chicago: Moody Press, 1978.

Saldarini, Anthony J. *Jesus and Passover.* New York: Paulist Press, 1984.

Sarna, Nahum. *The JPS Torah Commentary: Exodus.* Philadelphia: Jewish Publication Society, 1991.

_____. *The JPS Torah Commentary: Genesis.* Philadelphia: Jewish Publication Society, 1991.

_____. *Exploring Exodus: The Origins of Biblical Israel.* New York: Schocken Books, 1996.

Schauss, Hayyim. *The Jewish Festivals.* New York: Schocken Books, 1938.

Schiffman, Lawrence H. *Reclaiming the Dead Sea Scrolls.* New York: Doubleday, 1995.

Segal, Judah B. *Hebrew Passover from the Earliest Times to AD 70.* New York: Oxford University Press, 1963.

Shanks, Hershel. "Searching for Essenes at Ein Gedi, Not Qumran." *Biblical Archaeology Review* (July/August 2002).

Shanks, Hershel, ed. *Understanding the Dead Sea Scrolls.* New York: Vintage Books, 1993.

Silverman, David P. *Ancient Egypt.* Oxford: Oxford University Press, 1997.

Spangler, Ann and Lois Tverberg. *Sitting at the Feet of Rabbi Jesus.* Grand Rapids: Zondervan, 2009.

Taylor, Joan. "The Garden of Gethsemane: Not the Place of Jesus' Arrest." *Biblical Archaeology Review* (July/August 1995).

Telushkin, Rabbi Joseph. *The Book of Jewish Values.* New York: Bell Tower, 2000.

Tigay, Jeffrey H. *The JPS Torah Commentary: Deuteronomy.* Philadelphia: Jewish Publication Society, 1991.

Turkowski, L. "Peasant Agriculture in the Judean Hills." *Palestine Exploration Quarterly* 101 (1969): 101 – 12.

Tverberg, Lois with Bruce Okkema. *Listening to the Language of the Bible.* Holland, Mich.: En-Gedi Resource Center, 2004. *www.egrc.net.*

VanderKam, James C. *The Dead Sea Scrolls Today.* Grand Rapids: Eerdmans, 1994.

_____. *The Meaning of the Dead Sea Scrolls.* San Francisco: Harper Collins, 2004.

Vermes, Geza. *Complete Dead Sea Scrolls in English.* New York: Penguin Group, 1998.

Walsh, Carey Ellen. "God's Vineyard: Isaiah's Prophecy as Vintner's Textbook." *Biblical Archaeology Review* (August 1998).

Watterson, Barbara. *Gods of Ancient Egypt.* London: Sutton Publishing, 1996.

Wilkinson, Bruce. *Secrets of the Vine.* Colorado Springs: Multnomah, 2001.

Wilkinson, Richard H. *The Complete Gods and Goddesses of Ancient Egypt.* Hong Kong: Thames and Hudson, 2003.

_____. *The Complete Temples of Ancient Egypt.* Hong Kong: Thames and Hudson, 2000.

Wilson, Marvin. *Our Father Abraham: Jewish Roots of the Christian Faith.* Grand Rapids: Eerdmans, 1989.

Young, Brad H. *Jesus the Jewish Theologian.* Peabody, Mass.: Hendrickson, 1995.

Zevit, Ziony. "Three Ways to Look at the Ten Plagues." *Biblical Archaeology Review* (June 1990).

Zvi, Ron. "Agricultural Terraces in the Judean Mountains." *Israel Exploration Journal* 16 (1966).

More Great Resources
from Focus on the Family®

Volume 1: Promised Land

This volume focuses on the Old Testament—particularly on the nation of ancient Israel, God's purposes for His people, and why He placed them in the Promised Land.

Volume 2: Prophets & Kings of Israel

This volume looks into the life of Israel during Old Testament times to understand how the people struggled with the call of God to be a separate and holy nation.

Volume 3: Life & Ministry of the Messiah

This volume explores the life and teaching ministry of Jesus. Discover new insights about the greatest man who ever lived.

Volume 4: Death & Resurrection of the Messiah

Witness the passion of the Messiah as He resolutely sets His face toward Jerusalem to suffer and die for His bride. Discover the thrill the disciples felt when they learned of His resurrection and were later filled with the Holy Spirit.

Volume 5: Early Church

Capture the fire of the early church with the faith lessons in Vol. 5. See how the first Christians lived out their faith with a passion that literally changed the world.

Volume 6: In the Dust of the Rabbi

"Follow a rabbi, drink in his words and be covered with the dust of his feet," says the ancient Jewish proverb. Come discover how to follow Jesus as you walk with teacher and historian Ray Vander Laan through the breathtaking terrain of Israel and Turkey and explore what it really means to be a disciple.

More Great Resources
from Focus on the Family®

Volume 7: Walk as Jesus Walked

Journey to Israel where 12 disciples walked the walk their rabbi Jesus taught them. Examining the culture and the politics of the first century, Vander Laan opens up the Gospels as never before.

Volume 8: God Heard Their Cry

Just when it seemed that Pharaoh could not be defeated, God provided for His people in ways they never could have imagined. Join Ray in ancient Egypt for his latest study of God's faithfulness to the Israelites—and a promise that remains true today.

Volume 9: Fire on the Mountain

When the Israelites left Egypt, they were finally free. Free from persecution, free from oppression, and free to worship their own God. But with that freedom comes a new challenge—learning how to live together the way God intends. In this ninth set of Faith Lessons, discover how God teaches the Israelites what it means to be part of a community that loves Him, and the lessons we can begin to live out in our lives today.

Volume 10: With All Your Heart

Do you remember where your blessings come from? In Exodus, God warned Israel to remember Him when they left the dry desert and reached the fertile fields of the promised land. But in this tenth volume of Faith Lessons, discover how quickly the Israelites forgot God and began to rely on themselves.

Share Your Thoughts

With the Author: Your comments will be forwarded to the author when you send them to *zauthor@zondervan.com*.

With Zondervan: Submit your review of this book by writing to *zreview@zondervan.com*.

Free Online Resources at
www.zondervan.com

Zondervan AuthorTracker: Be notified whenever your favorite authors publish new books, go on tour, or post an update about what's happening in their lives at www.zondervan.com/ authortracker.

Daily Bible Verses and Devotions: Enrich your life with daily Bible verses or devotions that help you start every morning focused on God. Visit www.zondervan.com/newsletters.

Free Email Publications: Sign up for newsletters on Christian living, academic resources, church ministry, fiction, children's resources, and more. Visit www.zondervan.com/newsletters.

Zondervan Bible Search: Find and compare Bible passages in a variety of translations at www.zondervanbiblesearch.com.

Other Benefits: Register yourself to receive online benefits like coupons and special offers, or to participate in research.

ZONDERVAN®

ZONDERVAN.com/
AUTHORTRACKER
follow your favorite authors